LORING AND WYLE

SCULPTORS' LEGACY

FIGURE 26.
A corner of the studio, 1921. Photographer
unknown. Photo: gift of the Estates of Frances
Loring and Florence Wyle, 1983.

LORING AND WYLE
SCULPTORS' LEGACY

CHRISTINE BOYANOSKI

ART GALLERY OF ONTARIO
MUSÉE DES BEAUX-ARTS DE L'ONTARIO
TORONTO, CANADA

COVER:
Robert Flaherty, *Portrait, Frances Loring and Florence Wyle*, c. 1919; cyanotype, 14.6 × 14.7 cm. Art Gallery of Ontario, Toronto, gift of the estates of Frances Loring and Florence Wyle, 1983.

ISBN 0-919777-47-3

The Art Gallery of Ontario is generously funded by the Province of Ontario, Ministry of Citizenship and Culture.

Catalogue of an exhibition held at the Art Gallery of Ontario, Toronto July 24 - October 18, 1987

This exhibition is sponsored by Campeau Corporation.

Canadian Cataloguing in Publication Data
Boyanoski, Christine
    Loring and Wyle: sculptors' legacy

Catalogue to an exhibition held at the Art Gallery of Ontario, Toronto, July 24–Oct. 18, 1987.
Bibliography: p.
ISBN 0-919777-47-3

1. Loring, Frances, 1887-1968 — Exhibitions.
2. Wyle, Florence, 1881-1968 — Exhibitions.
I. Loring, Frances, 1887-1968. II. Wyle, Florence, 1881-1968. III. Art Gallery of Ontario. IV. Title.

NB249.L67A4 1987   730′.971′0740113541
C87-094464-9

TABLE OF CONTENTS

FOREWORD

Frances Loring and Florence Wyle were pioneers in the development of Canadian sculpture. Making Toronto their home in 1912, these women immediately became part of the city's art scene and worked in a converted church, often on the brink of poverty. Many of their sculptures are well-known and loved pieces seen throughout Toronto today.

Until now, the work of Loring and Wyle (and Canadian sculpture in general) has not been seriously studied or interpreted either for itself or within the broader context of Canadian art. This exhibition presents such an examination; it traces their creative development and recognizes Loring and Wyle as the truly great artists they were.

Campeau Corporation is honoured to sponsor this, the first retrospective of their work. For just as Loring and Wyle are known as pioneers in their field, so is Campeau Corporation, a major Canadian developer of commercial, income-producing properties throughout North America. Applauded for its award-winning office and retail developments, Campeau Corporation, a Canadian pioneer, is proud to make possible the first retrospective of the works of two truly gifted artists.

Robert Campeau
Chairman of the Board
Chief Executive Officer
Campeau Corporation

David King
President
Chief Operating Officer
Campeau Corporation

PREFACE

The Art Gallery of Ontario first showed the work of Florence Wyle and Frances Loring in 1915, when the institution was known as the Art Museum of Toronto. On a number of occasions through the years, the Gallery has presented their work in group exhibitions and in installations of our Permanent Collection; but it is the first time the Gallery has presented an exhibition exclusively devoted to the work of these two sculptors. The retrospective exhibition is supported by this publication, which documents their professional careers.

The specific occasion for the current exhibition is the celebration of the fact that the Art Gallery of Ontario has become the custodian of the estates of both artists. The gift from their estates included more than 180 sculptures, as well as photographs and documentary material, such as lists of their work, letters, and so on. In addition, a sum of money left in their estates has been made available to the Art Gallery of Ontario for the purchase of work by young Canadian sculptors. This purchase program will be administered by the Gallery's Canadian Contemporary Collection Committee in accordance with the wishes of the artists as expressed in their wills. To date, the Committee has purchased Liz Magor's *Four Boys and a Girl*, 1979.

This aspect of their wills came as no surprise to me; on several occasions, as we sat at late-afternoon tea in front of the fireplace in their studio, discussion turned on how their interest in and support for young Canadian sculptors could best be realized. It is therefore of great satisfaction to me, as Director, to see this project take practical form.

Aside from the very real artistic accomplishments of Florence and Frances, or "the Girls," as they were often called during their lifetimes, and the material legacy their bequest to the Gallery represents, their presence in Canada as practicing artists of outstanding commitment during most of this century demands our special respect.

In the epilogue of a biography called *The Girls*, written four years after their deaths by friend and fellow artist Rebecca Sisler, the author states, "The Girls had stood as beacons in the development of Canadian sculpture. Their own work reflected the school of art in which they were moulded, but their inspiration and direction came from life itself. The Girls' work in all instances was honest. They had absolute integrity within their conception. It was this integrity of spirit, coupled with a selfless devotion to the cause of artists that lifted their influence to a plane beyond that represented by their work alone."

The studio of the Girls was a principal centre in Toronto for artists, curators, critics and journalists to meet and discuss concerns of mutual interest with the sculptors and with each other. A.Y. Jackson is quoted as saying, "The art of Canada has, for many years, revolved around the studio of Frances Loring and Florence Wyle." It was second only to the Arts and Letters Club.

I would like to express the Gallery's thanks to the two executors of the Loring and Wyle estates—Frances Gage, sculptor, and David Ongley, solicitor—both long-time friends of the Girls. Their patience and guidance in settling the details of this important bequest to the Gallery was most appreciated.

Finally, I would like to thank Christine Boyanoski for this very handsome catalogue and for her detailed and enthusiastic research on the life and work of these very special women.

W.J. Withrow
Director
Art Gallery of Ontario

LENDERS TO THE EXHIBITION

Art Gallery of Ontario
John Brunke
Canadian Museum of Civilization
Canadian National Exhibition Archives
Canadian War Museum, Canadian Museum of Civilization
Concordia Art Gallery, Montreal
Alan Ely
Georgina Public Library
Marion Gibson

Lawrence Hayward
Mr. and Mrs. Donald Ketcheson
London Public Utilities Commission
London Regional Art Gallery
Charles McFaddin
The Honourable Pauline McGibbon
The McMichael Canadian Collection, Kleinburg
National Gallery of Canada, Ottawa
Mrs. R.H. Sankey

Sarnia Public Library and Art Gallery
Donald F. Scalzo, Winnetka, Illinois
Dr. and Mrs. Ben Schachter
T. Ormiston Smith, M.D.
Mr. and Mrs. Edward J. Stuebing
Catherine Thomas
The Winnipeg Art Gallery
Mr. Jennings Young
and four private collections

ACKNOWLEDGEMENTS

First and foremost, I would like to acknowledge the lenders, without whom this exhibition would not be complete. They have generously cooperated at all stages of its organization. As well, since many were personally acquainted with Loring and Wyle, they have provided me with valuable background information.

Since this exhibition was first conceived and research began in 1983, I have relied on a great many individuals for various forms of assistance and information; for the most part, primary source material provided the basis for my research. I would therefore like to begin this lengthy list with the editors of the journals and gallery newsletters who announced my search for information, and the many owners of Loring and Wyle sculpture who contacted me as a result. Many individuals, including members of the Loring and Wyle families, allowed me to view the works in their possession, or sent me photographs and descriptions. I would also like to thank the archivists and records managers: Christine Ardern and her staff in the Art Gallery of Ontario Archives; Larry Pfaff and Randall Speller of the E.P. Taylor Reference Library, Art Gallery of Ontario; Jim Burant, Anne Goddard, Louise Ouellette, and Norman M.

Willis at the Public Archives of Canada, Ottawa; Greg Spurgeon and Elaine Phillips at the National Gallery of Canada, Ottawa; Leon Warmski and Ken McPherson at the Archives of Ontario, Toronto; Nancy Hurn, Canadian National Exhibition Archives; Gerald Tooke, Royal Canadian Academy of Arts; Roy Schaefer, Osgoode Law Society Archives; Judith McErvel and Faye Wood, Eaton's Archives; Mrs. Hector McKnight, Women's Art Association; Judy Schwartz, Hart House; Peter Honor, Toronto General Hospital; Robert D. Mikel, Toronto Historical Board; Harold Averill, University of Toronto Archives; and Andrew Clarke, Corporation of the City of Cambridge.

I am also grateful for the generous help of my colleagues in other cultural institutions in Canada. At the National Gallery of Canada, Charles Hill, Curator of Canadian Art, Pierre Landry, Assistant Curator, and André Fronton, Registrar, provided valuable assistance, as did Judith Tomlin and Jean Soublière, History Division at the Canadian Museum of Civilization, and Hugh Halliday and Karen Graham at the War Museum in Ottawa. Renée P. Landry at the Canadian Centre for Folk Culture Studies and Kitty Glover of the Ethnology Department at the Canadian

Museum of Civilization are also to be thanked. The following individuals were also helpful: Judith Nasby, Director of the MacDonald-Stewart Art Gallery, Guelph; Andrew Oko in his former position as Curator of the Hamilton Art Gallery; Alan McNairn, Director of the New Brunswick Museum; Gary Essar, Associate Curator at the Winnipeg Art Gallery; Barry Fair of the London Regional Art Gallery, and Professor Leah Sherman at Concordia University. Special thanks are due to Ian Thom, Curator of the McMichael Canadian Collection, for bringing many relevant sources and works of art to my attention, and for acting as a sounding board for my ideas.

In the United States, the following individuals were especially helpful: James Mann of the Metropolitan Life Insurance Company, New York; Courtney Donnell, Judith Cizek, and Kathryn Vaughan at the Art Institute of Chicago and Roger Gilmore, Dean of the School of the Art Institute of Chicago; Maureen O'Brien Will at the Chicago Historical Society; Paula Kozol of the Museum of Fine Arts, Boston; Donna Hassler at the Metropolitan Museum of Art and Janis Connor of Conner-Rosencranz, New York City; Allen S. Weller of the Krannert Museum, Illinois;

Kay Miner, Waverly Public Library, Waverly, Illinois, and Charlotte Streifer Rubinstein, Laguna Beach, California.

For allowing me access to estate holdings of other Canadian sculptors, I wish to thank Qennefer Browne, executor of the Hahn/Wyn Wood Estate, and Angela Butler, a director of the Jacobine Jones Foundation. Robert Shipley allowed me access to his unpublished manuscript on Canadian war memorials, Penny Gray loaned me a copy of Christopher Chapman's 1965 film on the Girls made for the CBC programme *Telescope*, and Elspeth Chisholm generously sent me the typescript and notes of her 1956 interview with Frances Loring, the only extant records of this show in CBC's early *Profile* series. Both were invaluable for conveying the artists' thoughts.

I talked to many people who knew Loring and Wyle; I would particularly like to thank Elizabeth Gordon and Sophia Hungerford. Mr. and Mrs. Robert Sniderman were particularly cooperative in the initial stages of this project. I gained a deeper understanding of the technical realities of sculpting with the assistance of Judy Kuntz and George Boileau in night courses at the Ontario College of Art. In the final stages of research, Susan Marcus was helpful as my research assistant. I also wish to thank Pleasance Crawford, a landscape architect, and Arlene Gehmacher, a graduate student at the University of Toronto.

Within the Art Gallery of Ontario, the entire staff has provided valuable support for this exhibition and I appreciate their individual and collective contributions. The Graphic Design and Production Department, under Alan Terakawa, has been particularly involved, especially Steve Boyle, who has designed this handsome catalogue. I appreciated the constructive comments of contract editor Charis Wahl. The Technical Services Department, under Bernie Oldcorn, has worked extremely hard to present the works of art effectively, with the help of contract designer Heidi Overhill. Peter Gale, Head of Adult Programs, is also to be thanked. I am especially grateful to the Conservation Department under Sandra Lawrence, who undertook the tremendous task of restoring the sculpture, most of which required attention. She and her staff were assisted by student interns from the Sir Sandford Fleming Conservation Techniques Programme and the Queen's University Art Conservation Programme, and contract conservators Shelagh Youngs, Lynn Duncan-Smith, and Diane Falvey. The photography department, under head photographer Carlo Catenazzi, and with the able coordination of Faye van Horne, kept apace with the conservation. I also wish to thank Maia-Mari Sutnik, head of photographic services, whom I consulted on a number of occasions, and whose sustained enthusiasm for this project I appreciate. Alan Wilkinson, curator of modern sculpture, was helpful in suggesting sources of European sculpture and in lending me many of his own books on the subject.

Finally, I wish to acknowledge Dennis Reid, curator of Canadian historical art, for giving me the opportunity to work on this exhibition, from which I have gained invaluable experience, and for freeing me from my other regular duties for the past several months, enabling me to devote my energies entirely to this catalogue. He also read and commented on the manuscript. Our secretary, Leila Jamieson, never failed to provide me with capable and willing assistance in a cheerful manner, for which I am most grateful. David Ongley, solicitor, and Frances Gage, sculptor, deserve special thanks. They have given unselfishly of themselves over the years to help the Girls, both during the latter part of their lives, and after their deaths, as executors of their estates. I have consulted Frances Gage many times, and have benefited from her personal knowledge of the Girls, and her technical expertise in the field of sculpture. It has been a pleasure to work with them all.

Christine Boyanoski
Assistant Curator of Canadian Historical Art
February 1987

INTRODUCTION

The 1983 gift from the estates of Frances Loring and Florence Wyle to the Art Gallery of Ontario included a fine selection of their sculpture and a large number of photographs and personal papers. This combination makes the Gallery the major study centre for the work of these two women who made a major contribution to Canada's artistic heritage. Copyright for the reproduction of their work, both in photographic form and in three dimensions, has also been transferred from the estates to the Art Gallery of Ontario. The conception of this exhibition and the catalogue that documents it are direct results of this gift. This one large gesture made available to this institution a large representative body of the work of Loring and Wyle that could be carefully examined, documented, and restored over a period of time before being publicly presented.

The purpose of this exhibition is to display this splendid gift and to shed light on the collective and individual contributions of Frances Loring and Florence Wyle and to place their work within the context of Canadian, American and European sculpture of their day. The best examples from the gift are included, and more than half the works in this exhibition have been borrowed from outside sources, both public institutions and private individuals. This was to insure that the selection represent the breadth and high quality of their sculpture, in the most durable form wherever possible, and to indicate the extent to which the work has been disseminated. Items have been selected on the basis of aesthetic quality, frequency of exhibition, and historical significance, and with a consideration of known personal favourites of the sculptors themselves. The choice also reflects the availability of work. Florence Wyle is numerically better represented than Frances Loring for a number of reasons: she was a more prolific sculptor, and she kept most of her work, including maquettes. Loring destroyed much of hers. In addition, Loring worked primarily on architectural sculpture, which, for practical reasons, has been impossible to include in the installation; photographs have been substituted in three instances.

An examination of these two major protagonists of Canadian sculpture also makes possible a broader understanding of a previously neglected area in the history of Canadian art. Charles Band (1885–1969), an important collector and patron of the arts and one of the estates' executors, commented that, "Miss Loring and Miss Wyle are to Canadian sculpture what the Group of Seven is to Canadian painting." To understand their work is to understand in large part the history of Canadian sculpture. They have been neglected, until now, for several reasons. First, the production of academic sculpture has been difficult in this country because of lack of patrons and foundries; thus its history has not been a long one, and professional sculptors have been few. It is an art that demands physical strength and a large work space, more space than painters require. There are also financial considerations, not the least of which is the high cost of materials. A male artist with a family to support may have been less likely to make a career of sculpture than women like Frances Loring and Florence Wyle, who were willing to forgo traditional female roles and make personal sacrifices.

Sculpture has been called the "Cinderella of the Arts," defined as "something you back into at exhibitions while looking at the paintings." It requires more space to display a sculpture than a painting. Sculpture is also more demanding of the viewer than two-dimensional forms of art, partly because it intrudes physically on the viewer's physical space. Viewers may have unrealistic expectations before they approach the work, which may affect their appreciation of it, for even if the work realistically portrays something or someone known in real life, it is removed from reality, being a work of art. Even more traditional sculpture demands an appreciation of abstract form and a sensitivity to the displacement of space by volume. It often lacks the illusionism and sensuality offered by a painting, print, or drawing and, like theatre or opera, requires the suspension of disbelief.

While scholarship in the area of historical Canadian painting steadily advances, and while many individuals have done extensive research on Canadian sculpture, little has been published to date. American scholarship has been catching up in this field since the 1976 Bicentennial and many exhibitions are backed by fine publications and articles. Historical sculpture in Quebec has also received more attention than that of English Canada: there was a recent exhibition of Louis Jobin organized by the Musée du Qué-bec, and a new publication on early sculpture in Quebec by John Porter and Jean Bélisle. Several exhibitions in the past decade have included sculpture, set within the context of contemporary paintings, notably "Visions and Victories: Ten Canadian Women Artists 1914–1945," organized by the London Regional Art Gallery in 1983, but no sizeable exhibition has been devoted purely to sculpture. This exhibition of Frances Loring and Florence Wyle, the first ladies of Canadian sculpture, is a first.   C.B.

Notes on Technique

Sculpture is primarily an art of three dimensions. In its more traditional forms, it is made by modelling in a plastic material such as clay (an additive process), carving out of a solid mass (a subtractive process), or by assembling various materials, (as, for example, in the welding of metal). Throughout their careers, Frances Loring and Florence Wyle employed traditional techniques used by sculptors in the late-nineteenth and early-twentieth centuries. They carved extensively in wood in their later years; however, working directly in the material to create a unique piece was an idea to which the Girls did not generally subscribe. Even Wyle's *Cellist* (Cat. No. 61), her diploma piece executed first in mahogany, also exists in plaster.

Theirs was an art conceived of primarily in multiples. Because of the nature of production, which involves mould-making and casting, several pieces of sculpture can be created from the same original clay model; the final number cast in each edition is restricted only by the sculptor's wishes. By limiting the number of works in each edition, the sculptor is able to supervise each piece as it goes through the casting process, and ensure that the relatively rare quality of the work is preserved. As well, the multiple pro-cess makes the work available to more than one interested collector. For example, Frances Loring limited the number of castings of *Sir Frederick Banting* (Cat. No. 55, Pl. No. 3) to five, and when a sixth was requested, the permission of the original five owners was sought. Florence Wyle limited the number of castings of *Young Mother* (Cat. No. 45) to five; *Baby with Dolphin* (Cat. No. 29) to three; and *Torso* (Mother of the Race) (Cat. No. 48) to two bronzes and one marble. (The National Gallery of Canada owns the marble.) Another reason for limiting the numbers was that Loring and Wyle thought only five faithful copies could be had from one gelatin mould.

Almost no sketches or small rapid drawings on paper exist for the work of Loring and Wyle. Instead, they produced sketches called maquettes, which consist of small, rapidly modelled lumps of clay that contain the germs of ideas. After the roughly fashioned first sketch, a larger version that contains more detail may be cast in plaster. For example, such a maquette (Cat. No. 30) was entered in the initial stage of the National War Memorial Competition. Loring's maquettes for the *Osgoode Hall War Memorial* (Cat. No. 33) gave the Law Society of Upper Canada, which commissioned it, an idea of what the completed piece would look like. The maquette could also take the form of a more finished piece and could be exhibited as a completed work, as in the case of *Study of a Girl* (Cat. Nos. 32 and 50, Pl. No. 2). The smaller piece was used as a model in the enlargement process. Maquettes were used to establish main figural groupings, pose, and detail (See Cat. Nos. 91 to 94).

The next stage involved making a larger clay model, often half-size or life-size. The flexible material is applied to an armature, which is made of lead wire, wood, or wire mesh. The clay must be kept damp so that it will retain its flexibility and not crack, and also to facilitate its removal from the plaster mould. Photographs of the studio depict large forms swathed in wet sheets; it was particularly difficult to keep the clay moist in such an inadequately humidified space.

The clay model is then used to make a mould, either a waste mould, which is destroyed in the final casting process, or a piece mould, which can be used a number of times. The damp clay is surrounded by partially calcinated or dehydrated gypsum—plaster. The sculptor first spatters the clay model with plaster, then gradually builds up a thicker wall as the plaster

FIGURE 35.
Frances Loring with full-scale clay model of
Victory. Photographer unknown. Photo: gift of
the Estates of Frances Loring and Florence
Wyle, 1983.

begins to set. A piece mould is used when the sculpture has deeply undercut areas, which would be destroyed in casting; retaining walls of clay are built up to section off each individual piece of the mould. Once the mould is finished the clay model is removed, leaving its negative impression on the inside of the mould. The next step is to cast the work in plaster. If a piece mould has been used, the pieces are reassembled and bound together. Then liquid plaster is poured into the waste mould or the piece mould and left to set. The cast can be reinforced with burlap, chicken wire, or some form of fibre after the first coat of plaster has been applied. When the liquid plaster has set, the piece mould is disassembled. Or, in the case of a waste mould, the mould is chipped away to reveal the form, a replica in plaster of the original clay model.

It was usually this plaster cast that was displayed in exhibitions, with a patina painted on to indicate the permanent material the sculptor intended for the piece. By definition, patina refers to the film or incrustation, produced naturally by oxidation, that alters the surface of substances; a green patina is most common on bronze. A patina can be artificially induced through the application of chemicals and heat to the metal. In the case of plaster casts, an artificial patina is painted on to simulate the appearance of metal or stone. Various shades of green were used to indicate bronze (*Sir Robert Borden*, Cat. No. 93, or *The Miner*, Cat. No. 60); and a terra-cotta colour could signify stone

(*Bain Fountain Figure*, Cat. No. 72). Sealing the plaster with shellac, wax, or linseed oil, then applying an oil-based paint, also served to protect the work and to give the sculptor some idea of how it would look in permanent form. Unfortunately, all too often the work never got beyond the plaster stage. (That is why there are so few metal or stone sculptures and so many plaster casts.) When casts were made from the piece mould, the parting lines of the mould were often visible unless the sculptor refinished the surface of the plaster, or otherwise disguised the lines. (See *Study of a Girl*, Cat. No. 32, and *The Miner*, Cat. No. 60).

Works that did progress beyond plaster were delivered to a foundry or a stone carver. There were few foundries in Canada in the early years, and in Canada, none was considered trustworthy by the Girls. Even as late as 1964, Frances Loring advised a friend not to let anyone persuade her to have one of her works cast in Canada. "A head is too subtle a thing for them to handle," she wrote. Loring and Wyle had most of their casting done in the United States, at Gorhams or at the Roman Bronze Works, or else in Belgium, which was less expensive but took longer.

Two types of casting are possible at a foundry: the lost-wax method and sand casting. In the first instance, a gelatin piece mould is made from the plaster cast. The interior of the gelatin (modern foundries use vinyl) is coated to the thickness of about an eighth of

an inch with wax, which, when it is set, is removed from the mould. When it is assembled, it is an exact duplicate of the plaster cast. It is then filled with and surrounded by heat-resistant plaster. Then the entire unit is subjected to intense heat, which burns out the wax, leaving a hollow space, which will receive the molten bronze. (Sand casting differs from the lost-wax method only in the technique used to produce the wax model.) The sculptor checks the wax model, since the bronze will reproduce it exactly, including any bubbles or other flaws in its surface. The sculptor also checks the bronze once it is cast, to find any imperfections and to advise the foundry on the type of patina desired. The sculptor thereby retains control of the quality of the final product. (One must be wary of posthumous castings or castings in which the sculptor plays no part.) The bronze cast is twice removed from the clay model, and there is the danger that the subtleties of the sculptor's original concept could be lost. The plaster cast, of which there are many examples in this exhibition, is closest to the original concept.

With works to be carved in stone, the sculptor can also maintain some degree of control. He or she usually provides a professional stonecarver with a full-scale plaster model from which to rough out the work in stone to within a specified distance from the finished surface. The sculptor will then refine it to his or her liking. (See Wyle's *Sea and Shore*, Cat. No. 80.)   C.B.

FIGURE 1.
Florence Wyle at the Art Institute of Chicago, working on *The Spirit of the Mines*, c. 1910. Special Collections, E.P. Taylor Reference Library, Art Gallery of Ontario, Toronto. Gift of the Estates of Frances Loring and Florence Wyle, 1983.

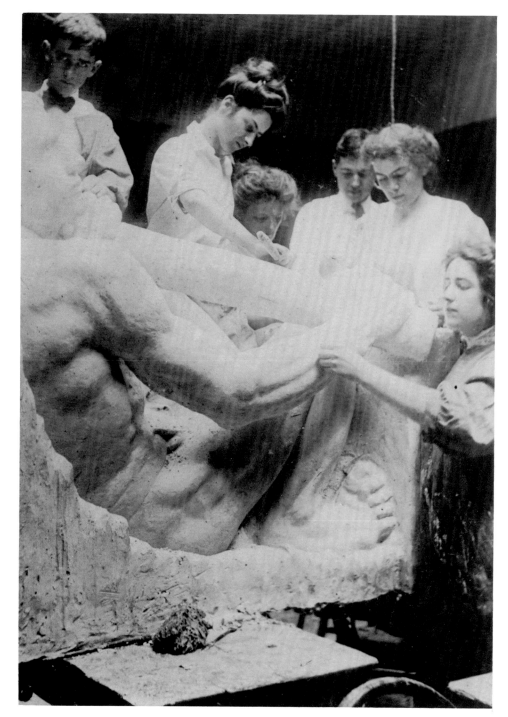

CONSERVATION OF THE SCULPTURE COLLECTION

While cast plaster provides the most faithful copy of an original, it is also one of the most fragile materials for sculpture. The surface, which may appear quite solid, is in fact relatively soft and prone to scratching, chipping, and water damage. The structure can be readily cracked or broken, in spite of the presence of metal armatures. In preparation for this exhibition, most of the plasters required some form of conservation treatment, ranging from cleaning and surface stabilization to structural repair to, in some cases, reconstruction or restoration.

Over the years, a number of the plasters had been stored in old studio spaces, garages, or basements where substantial dirt and grime built up on their surfaces. Thus the most common treatment was to clean the surface of the works with various aqueous- and solvent-based agents. At times this was complicated by the solubility of the paint or by a soluble paint patina, which was difficult to distinguish from the dirt.

Damage to the paint surface—scratches, gouges, chips, and flaking—were also common. The flaking, which involved actual lifting of the uppermost paint layers in flake-shaped segments, was treated by introduction of suitable consolidants to the affected area,

followed by gentle manipulation, to set the flakes back into position. Smaller scratches and chips were filled with fresh plaster, and, with other areas of missing paint, were toned, or "inpainted," for visual integration with the surrounding areas. Before we cleaned the plasters, we examined them, and we learned that the Girls frequently repainted their plaster sculptures, often with very different colours. The new paint may have been applied to cover surface damages and repairs, to refinish after casting, where the plaster had been used to prepare the mould, and sometimes to change the colour for a new exhibition of the work.

Other forms of surface cleaning proved more complicated. For example, *The Miner* (Cat. No. 60) and *The Old One* (Cat. No. 8) were encrusted by mould residues left after casting. Since the casting was posthumous, the artist had not repainted the work. It was left to the conservators to remove the residue mechanically, using fine needles and scalpels. Not all the mould could be removed without damage to the original surface. Thus, along with the clearly visible "parting lines," bits of mould material are still visible in indentations and crevices, giving the sculptures a very different appearance from the rest of the

collection. The large *Study of a Girl* (Cat. No. 50, Pl. No. 2) had been accidentally spattered with white paint, especially the head and right shoulder. Anything that dissolved the spatters also dissolved the underlying paint, so the hundreds of spatters were removed manually—one at a time.

More radical treatment was required for plasters that had suffered major damage or breaks. The baby of *Baby with Dolphin* (Cat. No. 29) was completely missing the big toe of his right foot. Fortunately, photographs provided adequate evidence to allow construction of a new toe. To distinguish the restoration from the original casting, the toe was painted a slightly different colour. In *Study for Sir Robert Borden (a)* (Cat. No. 91), the head had broken off at the neck; the figure was missing a right foot and the right section of the base. Attachment of the head with a stainless-steel dowel was quite straightforward, but the foot presented some problems. There was no photograph of the complete sculpture to work from. The base had to be completed to ensure stability of the sculpture; this was done first. Then, using the existing foot as a model and following the direction indicated by a fragment of heel, a new foot was carved in mirror image of the other. Once again, the colour of the restored area is slightly different from the original.

The small *Figural Grouping,* (Sketch for a war memorial) (Cat. No. 30) presented a problem: the soldier's head was missing. Again, there was insufficient photographic evidence for reconstruction. We had no idea of the features for a face, or even the angle of inclination for the head. Yet it was disturbing to view the work in its damaged state. The solution: to provide a temporary head shape, formed from tinted wax and loosely set onto the neck. From a viewing distance, the work presents a coherent image for interpretation, but the temporary restoration is clearly recognizable, and can be removed at any time.

A number of the works conserved for this exhibition were of materials other than plaster. Some of the carved wood pieces required only light surface cleaning, toning of the fine surface scratches, and, in some cases, securing of metal plaques. The small cast-iron bookends had all accumulated areas of surface rust, which was removed by gentle surface cleaning. Because of the presence of paint on these works, not all the rust could

be removed safely. *Birdbath* (Cat. No. 58), a life-size bronze, displayed problems similar to some of the plasters. After years out of doors, it had developed an uneven layer of surface corrosion—its natural patina. To disguise the corrosion, someone covered the work with a thick layer of black paint, which was, in turn, accidentally spattered with white paint at some point. Previous attempts had been made to remove the paint from the figure's left arm, with limited success. However, enough of the bronze surface was exposed to suggest that a full cleaning could be carried out. After several days of work, the original patinated surface was exposed, revealing subtle nuances of form that had long been hidden under the paint.

Several stone pieces had also suffered from years of exposure out of doors. One of the cast-stone *Blue Herons* (Cat. No. 31b), *Baby Fountain, Girl* (Cat. No. 42), and *Marble Fountain (Boy and Grapes)* (Cat. No. 1) had accumulated layers of caked dirt, leaves, tree resins, mould stains, and deposits of dried green algae. Washing of each work took a full day, with help from Technical Services staff to manipulate the heavy pieces (the

largest weighed more than seven hundred pounds) in the shower. Everyone got rather wet, but the results were most satisfying, even though some deep-set stains are still visible.

Modern or early-twentieth-century Canadian sculpture was very much a product of the times. Where expense and availability of materials so dictated, sculpture was produced in temporary fragile plaster. Alternatively, sculpture was commissioned for public areas or exterior landscape settings where time, nature, pollution, and vandalism have taken their tolls. The range of conservation treatments carried out for this exhibition generally reflect the problems encountered with much Canadian sculpture of this period. For the conservators who worked on the project, there is great satisfaction in having contributed to the preservation of a body of important work; and there is pleasure in seeing the pieces brought to a state more closely resembling their original appearance and perfection.

Sandra Lawrence
Chief Conservator

LORING AND WYLE
SCULPTORS' LEGACY

FIGURE 6.
Frances Loring, c. 1905. Photographer unknown.
Photo: gift of the Estates of Frances Loring
and Florence Wyle, 1983.

one

ARTISTIC TRAINING AND EARLY INFLUENCES

The names Frances Loring and Florence Wyle are inextricably linked in the history of sculpture in Canada and in the minds of those who knew them. Affectionately called "the Girls"[1] and known as the Loring-Wyles, they have always been thought of as team-mates whose work was so closely related as to be indistinguishable at times.[2] It was natural that they should be connected in this way because there were very few other women sculptors in Canada in the early years, and because they shared a studio, first in New York for three years (1909 to 1912), then in Toronto from 1914 until they were both hospitalized in 1966. They often competed with each other and with friends and colleagues for the few commissions available (the National War Memorial, 1925; the Metropolitan Life Insurance Company Competition, 1938). They would compete for some projects (relief panels for the Bank of Montreal, 1948, or the Calvert Drama Trophies, 1953) and collaborate on others (the Dominion Coat of Arms on the Customs Building, Niagara Falls, Ontario, 1941; a design for the memorial to King George VI, c. 1955). And there is evidence that their interaction was mutually beneficial to their creative development.[3]

Where similarities exist in their work, more often than not it is in terms of subject matter, which may have been specified in a particular commission and may simply reflect the spirit of the times. In actual fact, the stylistic differences in their work are striking and reflect their individual temperaments and the different paths their lives had followed (their mutual interest in sculpture aside) before Frances Loring met Florence Wyle at the Art Institute of Chicago in 1905. In short, Frances Loring considered herself primarily a sculptor of monuments and an architectural designer,[4] preferring to work on a large scale. Of her friend, Florence Wyle commented that she "didn't like to do pieces unless she had to climb a ladder to get at them."[5] Her sculpture bears the mark of an extrovert in its heroic scale and in the dynamic quality that energizes the best of her work. Florence Wyle was more concerned with pure form than dramatic effect, and had a better grasp of modelling and anatomy than her colleague. Stylistically, her work is more introverted and detached, more intimate in character, usually smaller in scale and more refined in treatment. A journalist in the 1920s perceived the work of Frances Loring as having "more emotion, a tenser drama in

line and movement," and something close to the "aching 'terribilitá' of Michel Angelo," and that of Florence Wyle as "quieter, more finished and reserved, more 'Greek.'"[6] Produced over a period of more than half a century as these women worked side by side, the sculpture of one acts as a perfect foil for the work of the other, illuminating it by contrast.

Florence Wyle was born on November 24, 1881, in Trenton, Illinois to Solomon B. Wyle and Libbie Sandford Wyle. According to Rebecca Sisler, Florence, her twin brother, Frank, and their three siblings were brought up in a strict patriarchal household in Waverly, Illinois where the family moved around 1884. It seems that Florence received encouragement only for the traditional female role, which confined her to the home, although she would have preferred to take her brother's place out of doors. She was resentful of these restrictions, which she felt to be unjust, and this affected her in adulthood. The persona she adopted later in life— a brusque manner and mannish dress—was her way of dealing with what she perceived to be the unfairness of being a woman in a man's profession, or, for that matter, in a man's world. These restrictions must have been

1

a great frustration for Florence, who, according to a former school chum, was an excellent student skilled at gymnastics and boxing.[7] It would have been with a feeling of liberation that she enrolled in a pre-medical course at the University of Illinois at Urbana in 1900, doubtless in the face of parental disapproval. Although she specialized in science, Wyle excelled in the anatomical drawing and sculpture courses that were part of the science curriculum.

There may have been some interaction between the medical schools and the Art Institute of Chicago by the 1890s. A course in anatomy for artists was offered by the Institute. However, unlike the Pennsylvania Academy of the Fine Arts in Philadelphia, it did not include dissection. However, the *Circular of Instruction* for 1892–1893 stated that arrangements could be made with the medical schools for those who wished to have this experience.[8] After three years, Wyle transferred to the School of the Art Institute of Chicago to pursue her growing interest in art. She was twenty-two years of age.

The next six years were spent at the Art Institute, first as a student, then as a teacher. The *Circular of Instruction* boasted that "the opportunities for the study of the human figure, which is universally regarded as the basis of the practice of art, are quite exceptional in the Art Institute." The school was also very proud of its department of modelling and sculpture, which it believed to be of "unusual importance." Under the practical guidance of Lorado Taft and Charles Mulligan, the students would "follow the usual routine of academic modelling of head and figure, and the composition of small groups, [and] compose and model draped figures, set up their own armatures, execute large figures, cut

marble, and in general perform the practical work of the studio." It was believed that in this way, they would be prepared for the actual practice of their profession. It was the only school in the United States at the turn of the century that taught student sculptors to carve in marble themselves. It was the usual practice for professional sculptors of the day to hand the plaster cast over to stonecarvers, who would transfer it into stone,[9] but the school felt that the student should have firsthand knowledge of the procedure.

Initially, Wyle studied drawing and painting, and took a course called "Life and Antique" with Frank Phoenix (a graduate of the Art Institute who had attended the Académie Julian, Paris) and John H. Vanderpoel (also a graduate of the Art Institute, and a former pupil of Louis Boulanger and Jules Lefebvre in Paris). While very few drawings of hers remain, apart from rapid sketches in notebooks,[10] there are a number of small oil sketches done both during a stay at the Gravenhurst Sanitarium in 1917 to 1918 and on a trip to British Columbia with the painter Anne Savage in 1927.

It does not appear that Wyle studied clay modelling during her first year at the school, but in the *Circular of Instruction* for 1904–1905 she is listed as a member of the life class and of the evening modelling class. The following year she continued in Vanderpoel's classes, working from the nude figure in the mornings, then studying modelling with Lorado Taft in the afternoons (Figure 1, p. xvi). She was also studying French. There is no indication that she graduated; however, the diploma was discontinued in some areas the very year she would have completed her course of study. (A diploma was seen as valuable only to graduates in architecture and design

and to those who wished to become teachers.) If Florence intended to become a professional sculptor, a diploma would not have been a requisite, which perhaps explains why she did not receive one.

Florence Wyle's association with the Art Institute continued for several years after the completion of her formal training. She taught modelling part-time from July 1906 until September 1909, sometimes as an assistant to Charles Mulligan (1866–1916), who became head of the sculpture department after Taft's retirement in 1906. Mulligan taught her how to cut marble: he had worked as a marble cutter in Chicago before meeting Taft and becoming the foreman of his workshop, which was set up to prepare for the 1893 World's Columbian Exposition.[11] Rebecca Sisler relates that Wyle regarded her relationship with Mulligan as a love affair of some depth and duration,[12] and he may have been one of the reasons she stayed on at the school.

By 1908, Wyle was well on her way to becoming established in the Chicago art world. She was settled in Oak Park, Illinois, a suburb of Chicago, in a house her mother had helped her to purchase, and where various family members boarded from time to time to help with the rent.[13] She began showing work in the Chicago Artists Exhibition that year, and executed a number of portraits, which may have been commissions, such as a head of Dr. David Monash, a physician and surgeon who instructed in obstetrics at Northwestern University Medical College. This work is known today only from a photograph.

Florence received the commission to design a drinking fountain for the Art Institute of Chicago from Newton Henry Carpenter, a former instructor at the institute, who was secretary there from 1881 to 1916. *Boy and Grapes* (Cat. No. 1) was installed in the south corridor of the institute in the summer of 1908, after it was shown in an exhibition called "Works by Chicago Artists" earlier that year. Designed and executed entirely by Wyle, it is an important work in her oeuvre for two reasons. First, she would return to the theme of a baby with a jug many times in her career (see, for example, Cat. No. 42); it is the type of work by which she first became known. Second, it is closely allied to work being done by contemporary American sculptors, particularly Janet Scudder (1872–1940). *Boy and Grapes* thus places Florence Wyle firmly in the tradition of American sculpture of the late-nineteenth and early-twentieth centuries.

Having placed Wyle within this tradition, something should be said of the nature of American sculpture in the first decade of the twentieth century. The Centennial Exhibition in Philadelphia in 1876 had made American artists more aware of French art, which was impressively represented there. Before the fair, American sculptors went *en masse* to Italy to find the schools and materials they needed to produce the idealized marbles then in demand (and which gave rise to the term "white marmorean flock"). The generation after 1876 was drawn instead to Paris, the undisputed centre of sculptural activity by the 1880s. It was in the art schools of Paris, and particularly at the Ecole des Beaux-Arts, that young Americans learned a new style, which satisfied the demand being made by a "Renaissance America" for an art of "bold naturalism and idealized imagery that would reflect its destiny, its aspirations, and its enormous pride and confidence."[14]

The first to meet this demand were Augustus Saint-Gaudens (1848–1907), Daniel Chester French (1850–1931), and Olin Warner (1844–1896), followed by Frederick William MacMonnies (1863–1937), Paul Wayland Bartlett (1865–1925), George Grey Barnard (1863–1938), and others. The Beaux-Arts style in which these sculptors worked was characterized by flickering surfaces and spontaneous modelling, a vigorous naturalism, and decorative qualities in both subject and form. The human figure remained the main vehicle of expression; often abstract concepts were represented through personification. The medium best suited to these stylistic qualities was bronze, which replaced marble as the predominant material for sculpture in the late nineteenth century.

Lorado Taft, Wyle's teacher at the Art Institute and the author of *The History of American Sculpture*, first published in 1903, acknowledged in his book that America owed the new spirit in sculpture to France, but hastened to add that the result was not French sculpture: "Paris has vitalized the dormant tastes and energies of America, that is all."[15] Cyrus E. Dallin (1861–1944), best known as a sculptor of the American Indian, who had been influenced by his training at the Académie Julian in Paris and by the noted French sculptor Henri Chapu (1833–1891), disagreed. In an article published in a Chicago art journal in 1903, entitled "American sculpture: its present aspects and tendencies," Dallin confessed that American sculpture was preeminently a reflection of France, and had not yet acquired a national character.[16] Perhaps Taft did not want to admit that the lessons of the French ateliers were not yet fully digested by American sculptors, for he had been responsible for bringing the French

sculptural tradition to the Art Institute of Chicago: he had studied in Paris at the Atelier Thomas in the first half of the 1880s.[17]

Florence Wyle did not study in France, but she was exposed to the Beaux-Arts tradition by her two teachers. (Mulligan had been a student of Alexandre Falguière, 1831–1900.) She travelled to England, France, and Belgium for the first time in 1924 and, when questioned in the 1940s as to how these travels had influenced her work, she replied that they had "made her more satisfied with this side of the Atlantic."[18] In any case, her early work was more closely allied with more immediate sources; namely, works by contemporary Americans whose sculpture could at times be very French indeed. The best example of this is *Dancing Boy*, from about 1910 (Cat. No. 2).

Dancing Boy was exhibited frequently in the early years, and it is possible that more than one bronze was cast.[19] When it was first shown at the Winter Exhibition of the National Academy of Design held at 215 West Fifty-seventh Street (now the Art Students League Building) in New York City in December 1910, a reviewer described it as having "grotesque but graceful abandon."[20] In pose and buoyant spirit, as well as in modelling, the work shares much with Frederick MacMonnies' infamous *Bacchante with an Infant Faun* 1893 (Figure 2), a cast of which was removed from the courtyard of the Boston Public Library soon after it was placed there and offered to the Metropolitan Museum of Art in New York, where it currently resides. Reductions were later made, as well as a full-scale replica for the Luxembourg Museum in Paris. Its "frivolous" quality appealed to the French, who were accustomed to works such as one by Hippolyte Moulin (1832–

FIGURE 2.
Frederick William MacMonnies. *Bacchante with an Infant Faun*, 1893. Bronze. The Metropolitan Museum of Art, New York, Gift of C.F. McKim, 1897. (97.19)

1884), *A Lucky Find at Pompeii*. Made after 1863, it was typical of French Salon sculpture of the period in that it was an exotic genre subject and an adolescent in an active, unconventional pose. A critic of the 1864 Salon noted that the best statues stood only on one foot.[21]

Wyle's *Dancing Boy* is more awkward in pose than its forerunners; he appears unstable, and the uncomfortable disposition of his arms, which embrace the space before him, is more suggestive of an attempt to regain his balance than a purposeful gesture related to a dance. Wyle's intention to create a sinuous Art Nouveau silhouette by positioning the limbs in this manner has resulted in an awkward tension. She was more successful in a later version of a dancing child executed around 1928 for Lady Eaton (Figure 3).

The sculptor whose work Wyle's most closely resembles was Janet Scudder, who was born at Terre Haute, Illinois, and worked in the studio of Lorado Taft around the time of the Chicago World's Fair. She was one of Taft's "White Rabbits," the name given to Taft's corps of female assistants. (By the 1890s, there were many female sculptors in the United States, probably because art schools opened their doors to women during the previous decade, and because of the growing popularity of small bronzes, which provided women with unprecedented opportunities to become sculptors.[22] One may assume that the intimacy, informality, and freedom from the standard subject matter of monumental works attracted women to the medium, as would the greater ease of working on a smaller scale. The careers of Loring and Wyle began in the wake of this trend.)

After she worked for Taft, Scudder studied with Frederick MacMonnies in Paris. His example provided her with an alternative to

creating ponderous public monuments; she preferred to sculpt pleasing, light-hearted works. She achieved this in the many fountain figures of children for which she is best known, such as the *Frog Fountain*, 1901 (Metropolitan Museum of Art, New York), which features a small boy balancing on one foot surrounded by three frogs from whose open mouths spout small jets of water. Wyle's *Baby* (Cat. No. 11), a portrait done in 1915, is exactly the type of sculpture Scudder was doing at that time.

Florence Wyle's early work may also be compared to that of the most noteworthy American Beaux-Arts sculptors, Daniel Chester French and Augustus Saint-Gaudens. Winged personifications were an integral part of French's new ideal imagery, used to express abstract concepts, as in *The Angel of Death and the Sculptor* (the Milmore Memorial), which is in the Metropolitan Museum of Art. Wyle used this imagery in her *Angel of the Pool* (c. 1910; Figure 4, p. 68), also known as "Spirit of the Spring," or "Angel—Memorial Fountain", a piece that has been lost. However, Florence Wyle's greatest strength as a sculptor is revealed in her portraits in shallow relief, and one of the finest is called *F.C. Loring*, done in the 1920s (Cat. No. 40). An exemplar was to be found in the work of Augustus Saint-Gaudens, master of the shallow relief, whose experience as a cameo cutter no doubt contributed to his skill. No artist interested in this difficult medium could have been unaware of his virtuoso portraits (Figure 5). The shallow relief, halfway between drawing and sculpture, is probably the most difficult type of sculpture to achieve successfully. The effect depends upon subtle modelling; form is defined by contrasts in light and shadow created by slight shifts in plane. Perhaps Wyle spent so long in

John Vanderpoel's drawing and painting classes to attain the proficiency at drawing required in the production of reliefs. The reliefs in this exhibition, particularly those that do not use polychromy, illustrate her skill in this demanding art form; for in works such as *Edward Kendall* (Cat. No. 17), she did not require colour to define form. In the relief of *Ethel Ely* (Cat. No. 27) colour merely serves a decorative purpose.

Florence Wyle was consistently nurtured by her long association with the Chicago Art Institute and guided by the example of more established artists like Saint-Gaudens, MacMonnies, Scudder, and others; her artistic heritage as well as her geneology were thoroughly American. She must have felt some pride in her American roots; although Frances Loring became a naturalized Canadian in 1926, Wyle retained her American citizenship all her life.

Whereas the artistic training and influences in Florence Wyle's life followed a continuous thread, the opposite is true of Frances Loring. Born in the United States, she received a large portion of her training in Chicago, Boston, and New York. But she had a much broader range of experiences than Wyle. She moved frequently with her family (her father was a mining engineer), and she benefited from direct exposure to European art early in life. Unlike Loring, she was encouraged in her interests by a supportive father who adored her and to whom she was very close.

Frances Norma Loring (Figure 6, p. xx) was born in Wardner, Idaho, on October 14, 1887 to Charlotte Moore and Frank Curtis Loring. Frances lived in Spokane, Washington from 1891 until 1899, the year Frank Loring moved to New York City and sent his wife, son Ernest and daughter Frances to Europe

FIGURE 3.
Florence Wyle, *Dancing Baby*, c. 1928. Plaster, location unknown, Photo by Pringle and Booth Limited. Special Collections, E.P. Taylor Reference Library, Art Gallery of Ontario, Toronto. (Henceforth cited as "Photo: gift of the Estates of Frances Loring and Florence Wyle, 1983.") Gift of the Estates of Frances Loring and Florence Wyle, 1983.

FIGURE 5.
Augustus Saint-Gaudens. *Jules Bastien LePage*, 1880. Bronze, 37.0 x 26.2 cm. Museum of Fine Arts, Boston, Everett Fund.

FIGURE 7.
Walter Allward. *The Bell Telephone Memorial*,
Brantford, Ontario, central relief, 1917.
Bronze. Photo possibly by M.O. Hammond.
Special Collections, Edward P. Taylor Reference
Library, Art Gallery of Ontario.

with the returns from good financial invest-
ments. A sudden change in fortune resulted
in the family being stranded in Europe until
Frank Loring could afford to bring them back
to the United States in 1905. During this
period, Frances lived and studied in some of
the major European artistic centres: at the
Ecole des Beaux-arts in Geneva, Switzerland
(1901–1903), in the Munich studio of a
Professor Guttner (1903–1904) and at the
Académie Colarossi in Paris (1904–1905).
When the family returned to the United
States, Frances Loring was seventeen.

The European sojourn gave Loring an
exposure to current European art at an age
when she was able to appreciate the experience. It was in the venerable art schools of
Europe that she was first introduced to sculpture, and it was here that her perceptions
of the art were first formed. While probably
not having any specific influence on her
artistic formation, these experiences

undoubtedly had a lasting effect on the
impressionable adolescent. Most telling of
this exposure is the element of symbolism
present in her work, a characteristic shared
by other sculptors trained in Europe at the
time; the chief exponent of this symbolism in
sculpture was Auguste Rodin. This symbolism, in which the form and movement of the
human figure is used to convey an idea or
emotion, and is exemplified by Loring's *Grief*
(Cat. No. 15), seems to have been absent
in Wyle's early work. On the other hand,
Loring was predisposed to this form of artistic
expression by nature, and something of her
approach to art may have rubbed off on Wyle
after they met.

The most influential sculptor in Europe at
the turn of the century was undoubtedly
Rodin. This was recognized in the literature
of art at that time.[23] Simply stated, three
features of Rodin's art were influential. First,
the poses of his figures, which he used to
express human emotions. Second, his choice
of themes, which were often from the Middle
Ages, or from the work of the Romantic
poets, who drew on similar sources. Among
Rodin's best-known works are *The Burghers of
Calais* (1884–1895), based on an event from
French mediaeval history, and *The Gates
of Hell*, commissioned by the French government in 1880 as the portal for a new Museum
of Decorative Arts, which was based on
Dante's *Inferno*. The gates were first exhibited
in an unfinished state (they remained in
plaster even at his death) in 1900. The third
influence was the unfinished quality of his
work, or "non-finito," where an academically
finished figure would be contrasted with its
base, which had been left in a rougher state.
The figure would appear to emerge from the
mass of the material in much the same way as
Michelangelo's figures do, particularly his

6

FIGURE 9.
Frances Loring. *Fountain*, c. 1908. Plaster,
location unknown. Photo: gift of the Estates of
Frances Loring and Florence Wyle, 1983.

FIGURE 10.
Frances Loring. *Sundial*, c. 1908. Plaster, location
unknown. Photo: gift of the Estates of Frances
Loring and Florence Wyle, 1983.

slaves for the tomb of Julius II, which appear
to struggle within the stone. Michelangelo
is the ultimate source for this mannerist approach to sculpture. The expressive qualities
created by finishing some parts of a block
of stone more than others, appealed to sculptors of Rodin's generation.[24]

Unfortunately, none of Frances Loring's
large early pieces, in which the influence
of Rodin is most apparent, are known to have
survived; they are known today only from
photographs. In 1908, the same year Florence
Wyle executed the marble fountain for the
Art Institute of Chicago, Frances Loring
exhibited *Fountain* (Figure 9) and *Sundial*
(Figure 10) at the Canadian National Exhibition. *Fountain* is a male figure, stretched out
on his stomach and leaning over a rocky
promontory, his hands cupped to catch a
stream of water. The smooth finish of the
naked body is accentuated by its direct contact
with the less finished rock-like base. One is
reminded of Rodin's *Danaid* of 1888, in the
Musée d'Orsay, Paris. *Sundial* is reminiscent
of Rodin's *Fallen Caryatid Carrying Her Stone*
(1881, Musée Rodin, Paris), a figure from
his *Gates of Hell* to which his *Crouching
Woman* is also related (Figure 11). Loring's
kneeling figure, *Grief*, first exhibited at the

joint exhibition of the Royal Canadian
Academy (RCA) and the Ontario Society of
Artists (OSA) in April 1918, similarly expresses
an intense emotional state. The figure's head
is bent forward, her hand clutching her breast.
The folds in her garment meld into the
pitted ground on which she kneels so that
figure and earth are in sympathy; her smoothly
modelled bare feet, however, are set effectively against this same ground, and gain in
expressiveness as a result. The piece may
have been created in response to the First
World War.

Other Canadian sculptors trained in Europe
at the turn of the century were also influenced by Rodin. In *Le Rêve Brisé* (Figure 12)
by Alfred Laliberté (1878–1953), first shown
at the 1911 Royal Canadian Academy annual
exhibition, an allegorical female figure lifts
the veil of sleep from her face. The sculptor
has skilfully varied the degree of finish so

FIGURE 11.
Auguste Rodin. *Crouching Woman*, 1880–1882.
Bronze, H. 95.3 cm. Art Gallery of Ontario,
Toronto. Anonymous Loan.

FIGURE 12.
Alfred Laliberté. *Le Rêve Brisé*, c. 1911. Marble,
L. 41.9 cm. Art Gallery of Ontario, Toronto.
Purchase, 1984.

as to fully exploit the beauty of the marble. The smooth sensuality of the woman's back and the diaphanous quality of the veil are heightened by contrast to the base, where the marks of the rasp have been left unpolished. Laliberté had studied in Paris around 1900 at the Ecole des Beaux-Arts. One finds a similar concern for the expressive use of form in the early work of Emanuel Hahn (1881–1957), a contemporary of the Girls. Hahn taught sculpture at the Central Ontario School of Art from 1910, and would be a cofounder of the Sculptors' Society of Canada in 1928. In *Man and Woman*, c. 1910 (Figure 13), the symbolism of the destiny shared by the couple is conveyed through the modelling of their forms, which rise united out of an irregular base treated as an integral part of the composition. Hahn, who was born in Wurtemberg and brought to Canada as a child, returned to Germany, where he studied at the Kunstgewebeschule and at the Kunstacademie und Polytechnikum in Stuttgart around 1905.

Florence Wyle could not have been unaware of Rodin and his followers, but it was not until she began sharing a studio with Frances Loring in New York City in the fall or winter of 1909 that her work took on an expressive quality, which it previously lacked. The two women met in Lorado Taft's modelling class at the Art Institute of Chicago. Frank Loring had opened an office in Chicago in 1905,[25] and his family must have joined him there upon returning to America. Frances spent only one year at the Art Institute, but, as Rebecca Sisler has noted, she and Florence "clicked" immediately.[26] While in Chicago, Frank Loring was attracted by reports of the Cobalt silver district in northern Ontario, and moved there in February 1906. Frances spent the academic year 1906–1907

at the School of the Museum of Fine Arts in Boston, where she studied modelling with Bela Lyon Pratt (1867–1917),[27] but she joined her family in Cobalt in the summer. Florence Wyle was invited there as a summer guest. After visiting Toronto briefly in 1908, where she showed work in all the major annual exhibitions (the OSA, RCA and the CNE),[28] Frances Loring decided to move to New York City, perhaps after visiting her father, who resided there for a brief period in 1909.[29] She was joined there late that year or early in 1910 by Florence Wyle.

NEW YORK CITY 1909–1912

In the thirteenth census of population for the city of New York, taken on April 27, 1910, Loring and Wyle are recorded as living at 6 Macdougal Alley with Loring's mother, Charlotte, and are described as "sculptors working on their own account" (Figure 14). Macdougal Alley is located in the heart of Greenwich Village—a cul-de-sac lined with coach houses that once belonged to the fashionable houses of Washington Square, which back onto it. Greenwich Village was rapidly becoming the focus of artistic life in

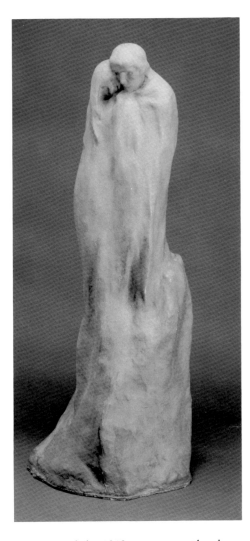

and Gertrude Vanderbilt Whitney, founder of what would become the Whitney Museum, who moved to the alley and began her career as a sculptor in 1907. Macdougal Alley was already reputed to be an artists' colony in 1906, when it was the subject of a feature article in *The Craftsman*.[31]

Number 6 was a converted stable with additional living space located in the loft above (Figure 15). In this studio, in 1911, Loring and Wyle did the well-known portraits of each other (Cat. Nos. 4 and 5). They are realistic portraits that faithfully describe how they appeared at that time: both wore their long hair braided and arranged softly around the crown of their heads so it would not get in the way of their work. Towards the end of the First War, Florence had her hair cropped in a style she wore for the rest of her life. During this period, they also began fashioning works for a commercial market; objects such as ornamental table-top bronzes (Cat. No. 3), paper knives (Cat. No. 7), candlestick holders (Cat. No. 6), and clock cases (Cat. No. 10) were shown in both the Tiffany and Gorham showrooms. These objects, which wed design with function, catered to the prevailing taste for Art Nou-

FIGURE 13.
Emanuel Hahn *Man and Woman*, 1905–1910. Plaster, H. 61 cm. Art Gallery of Ontario, Toronto. Purchase 1981.

FIGURE 14.
Macdougal Alley, c. 1910. Standard Photo Illustrating Company, New York. Photo: gift of the Estates of Frances Loring and Florence Wyle, 1983. Number 6 is on the extreme right.

FIGURE 15.
Interior of the Macdougal Alley studio, c. 1910. Standard Photo Illustrating Company, New York. Photo: gift of the Estates of Frances Loring and Florence Wyle, 1983.

the city, and, by 1912, it was considered the equivalent of the Parisian Left Bank, with a "strong whiff of artistic Bohemia tincturing its air."[30] By the time the Girls moved in, most of the other residents of the alley were artists—notably Edwin W. Deming, a painter and sculptor from Ohio; James Earle Fraser, the sculptor who taught modelling at the Art Students League, which Frances attended;

FIGURE 16.
Harriet Whitney Frishmuth. *Pushing Men, A Pair of Bronze Book-ends*, 1912. Bronze, H. 19.8 cm. Photo courtesy of Christies, New York.

FIGURE 17.
Florence Wyle. *The Sacrifice*, c. 1915. Plaster, location unknown. Photo: gift of the Estates of Frances Loring and Florence Wyle, 1983.

veau.[32] Frances Loring chose the highly popular peacock motif for her clock, while Florence Wyle, like most sculptor-craftsmen of the day, continued to use the human figure even in the decorative arts, in her caryatid candlesticks. Here, the figures visually describe the function performed by the object, just as Harriet Whitney Frishmuth's "Pushing Men" book-ends of 1912 describe theirs (Figure 16). Wyle continued to make candlesticks and book-ends throughout her career; the design changed with the times (Cat. Nos. 36 to 38).

Wyle's candlesticks are reminiscent of Rodin's *Thinker* and his caryatid from *The Gates of Hell*. His influence is also apparent in later, more significant pieces, such as the *Sun Worshipper* (Cat. No. 14), perhaps a paraphrase of Rodin's *Prodigal Son*, one of the figures for *The Gates* that had been cast separately; *Rebirth*, first shown in 1914 at the Annual RCA Exhibition; and *The Sacrifice* (Figure 17), which bears a stylistic resemblance to some of Frances Loring's work. This affinity to Rodin, and the emotive quality newly infused into Wyle's work, may have been the result of sharing a studio with Frances Loring.

Like many late-nineteenth and early-twentieth century artists, the Girls were inspired by the Romantic poets. Frances Loring sculpted two figures in New York based on literary sources: *Lamia* (Cat. No. 3), from a poem by John Keats, and *A Dream within a Dream* (Cat. No. 16),[33] from a work by Edgar Allan Poe.[34] Around 1916, Wyle sculpted *Pot of Basil*, her only known work directly inspired by a poem—Keats's "Isabella; or, The Pot of Basil." With its source in Boccaccio's *Decameron*, this popular subject was treated by a number of artists in the nineteenth century.

Considering their steady production, and their happy situation in the heart of a lively artistic colony, it is curious that Loring and Wyle left New York, probably late in 1912.[35] According to their biographer, Frank Loring was anxious that his daughter join the rest of the family in Canada, or perhaps that she not live in New York, and took it upon himself to shut down their studio when both women were absent.[36] Frances later explained her reasons for coming to Canada differently: "I started my artistic career in New York, but I prefer to be a big fish in a small pool, so I came to Canada."[37] She also said: "My father's activities as a pioneer mining engineer and his vision of Canada's future was probably a great influence upon my faith in the possibilities of Canada's growth artistically, also in my preference to be part of the development of a young country."[38] In a 1956 interview, she stated that it was exciting to live and work in Canada, "where you feel you're in on the beginnings of things," and that she wouldn't live anywhere else.[39] That Loring thought in such heroic terms is evident in her work, done in the fifty years that followed, and, indeed, this pioneering spirit was needed by a woman sculptor in Canada in 1913.

ENDNOTES

1. This was how they were known to their friends. Similarly, the photographers Charles Ashley and James Crippen were known as "the Boys." They offered mutual support in a cultural environment that gave little encouragement to sculptors, and each balanced the other's personality— Loring was a natural leader with a dominant personality from which the more reticent Wyle drew strength.

2. Irene B. Hare's article in *Sunday World* (May 25, 1924), entitled "Close-ups of Toronto's Women Sculptors: No. 1: Miss Frances Loring and Miss Florence Wyle," was one of the first to focus on their artistic relationship. Later articles included "Women with Mallets: Loring and Wyle complete three decades of partnership in sculpture" (*New World Illustrated*, February 1942) and "Unique Church Studio is Home and Workshop for Loring and Wyle, Canadian Sculpture Team" (*Saturday Night*, November 18, 1944).

3. In a film directed by Christopher Chapman for the Canadian Broadcasting Corporation's programme *Telescope*, first aired in May 1965, host Fletcher Markle asked Frances Loring if there was any cross-influence in their work. Loring replied, "In contrary ways," indicating that any suggestion by one would result in a contrary action by the other. Earlier she had stated: "The longer Miss Wyle and I work together, the stronger and more definite our styles become. We criticize each other's efforts vigorously and frankly— no, bluntly is the word." (John R. Lewis, "Why would a woman want to be a sculptor?" *Star Weekly Magazine*, January 2, 1960).

4. Completed questionnaire for *Who's Who in American Art* received by the National Gallery of Canada, September 1946. Lawrence Hayward Collection, Documentary Art and Photography Division, Public Archives of Canada, Accession No. 1973-19.

5. Rebecca Sisler, *The Girls* (Toronto and Vancouver: Clarke, Irwin and Company Limited, 1972), p. 29.

6. Arthur E. McFarlane, "Art Awakes in a Forgotten Church," *Toronto Star Weekly*, August 1, 1925.

7. "The Story of a Waverly Artist," *Waverly Journal*, December 21, 1945.

8. Roger Gilmore, ed., *Over a Century: A History of the School of the Art Institute of Chicago 1866–1981* (Chicago: The School of the Art Institute of Chicago, 1982), pp. 70–71, n. 25.

9. Gilmore, p. 72, and *Circular of the Art Institute of Chicago*, 1905–1906, pp. 28–29.

10. One notebook is contained in the Lawrence Hayward Collection, Archives of Ontario; another, dated 1920–1938, is in the collection of the National Gallery of Canada, Ottawa (28,168).

11. Taft had been appointed supervisor for the enlargement of sculptural decoration at the World's Columbian Exposition, an awesome task, considering the amount of monumental sculpture contained within the "White City."

12. Sisler, *The Girls*, p. 18.

13. Letter to the writer from Janet von Dach, a grand-niece of Florence Wyle, dated December 10, 1985.

14. Wayne Craven, *Sculpture in America*, rev. ed. (Newark: University of Delaware Press), p. 373. The term "American Renaissance" describes a period in the cultural history of the United States from 1876 to 1915–1917.

15. Lorado Taft, *The History of American Sculpture* (New York: Arno Press, 1969), reprint of the revised edition, p. 9.

16. Cyrus E. Dallin, "American Sculpture: its present aspects and tendencies," *Brush and Pencil*, Vol. 2, No. 6 (March, 1903), p. 424.

17. In the extensive correspondence that has survived from his student years, Taft never once mentions Auguste Rodin (1840–1917), the most influential sculptor of his day. Rather, he lavishes praise on Marius-Jean-Antonin Mercier, Paul Dubois, and Alexandre Falguière. Rodin's influence, however, is evident in his later work, as well as in the work of his students. What Esther Sparkes has termed "the figure-emerging-from-the-mass mannerism" was characteristic of his immediate students (*A Biographical Dictionary of Painters and Sculptors in Illinois 1808–1945*, PhD Dissertation for Northwestern University, 1971), and he was supportive of other artists working in this mode, George Grey Barnard, for example. Also, the large figural groupings he assigned to his students is reminiscent of Rodin's *Burghers of Calais* (1884–1895). A cast of one of these figures entered the collection of the Art Institute of Chicago in 1893.

18. A 1942 questionnaire completed for the University of Toronto Schools. National Gallery of Canada Archives: Artists' Correspondence File 7.1-W.

19. The same piece was exhibited both at the 40th Annual OSA in Toronto (March 9–30, 1912) and the 16th Annual Exhibition of the Society of Western Artists held in Chicago (March 5–27, 1912). A bronze was shown in Chicago; perhaps

it was the plaster cast that was in the Toronto show.

20. "Sculpture important in the National Academy Exhibition for the winter of 1910," *The Craftsman* (New York), Vol. 19, No. 5, February 1911, p. 452. According to the article, this was the first time in the history of the academy that an entire gallery had been devoted to sculpture. The Winter Exhibitions, like the Academy Annuals, were advertised juried shows, that attracted submissions by many artists who, like Wyle, were not necessarily members.

21. *A Lucky Find* is illustrated in *The Romantics to Rodin* (Los Angeles: Los Angeles County Museum of Art, 1980), p. 308; and in *Nineteenth Century French Sculpture: Monuments for the Middle Class* (Louisville: J.B. Speed Art Museum, 1971), p. 202.

22. *The Woman Sculptor: Malvina Hoffman and her contemporaries* (New York: Berry-Hill Galleries, Inc., 1984), essay and catalogue by May Brawley Hill, p. 6. According to art historian Charlotte Streifer Rubinstein, the Midwest was more open and egalitarian than other parts of the United States. Its land-grant colleges were making low-cost art education available to women.

23. An article by the poet Camille Mauclair was published in August 1901 in the *Revue Universelle* entitled "Auguste Rodin: son oeuvre, son milieu, son influence." In the entry on French sculpture in the eleventh edition of the *Encyclopaedia Britannica*, Vol. 24, p. 510, published in 1911, the author, Léonce Bénédite, keeper of the Musée National du Luxembourg, Paris, recognized Rodin to have had the most vital influence on modern sculpture in France and on many foreign schools.

24. Michelangelo was popular with turn-of-the-century sculptors in Canada, also. The recumbent male figure in Walter Allward's *Bell Telephone Memorial* (Figure 7) is a paraphrase of Michelangelo's Adam from the Sistine ceiling. A photograph of the first studio Loring and Wyle shared in Toronto from 1914 to 1920 (Figure 8, p. 14) shows a reproduction of this same figure tacked to the wall. Wyle later maintained that the sculptors who had most influenced her work were "Michelangelo and the Greeks."

25. His business address was listed in the 1905–1906 city directory as the Monadnock Block.

26. Sisler, *The Girls*, p. 20.

27. What drew her to Boston is unknown; however, her brother Ernest was studying engineering at MIT at that time.

28. She exhibited with them all, probably through the OSA, since the Annual Exhibition of the RCA was held at the OSA Gallery a month after the OSA show had closed, and the OSA had agreed to "undertake the conduct of the Art Gallery of the CNE as in previous years." (Minutes of the Executive Council Meeting of the OSA, June 2, 1908, p. 266, Archives of Ontario.)

29. Frank Loring is listed in *Trows General Directory of the Boroughs of Manhattan and the Bronx* at 618 West One Hundred Fourteenth Street for 1909–1910 only.

30. Allen Churchill, *The Improper Bohemians: A re-creation of Greenwich Village in its Heyday* (New York: E.P. Dutton, 1959), p. 22.

31. P.T. Farnsworth, "The Artists' Colony in Macdougal Alley, where some of our best-known American painters and sculptors live and work," in *The Craftsman*, Vol. 11, No. 1 (October, 1906), pp. 57–69. My thanks to Donna Hassler, of the Department of American Paintings and Sculpture at the Metropolitan Museum of Art in New York, for making this article known to me.

32. The Girls would have been fully conversant with this style: a Glasgow School exhibition was held at the Art Institute of Chicago in 1906; the student magazine *The Sketchbook* was filled with articles illustrating the current interest in Art Nouveau design; and Alphonse Mucha lectured and taught at the school from 1907–1909.

33. The marble version was carved later. See Sisler, *The Girls*, p. 22 and p. 63. It was identified as marble when it was exhibited in the *Annual Exhibition of Canadian Art* held at the National Gallery of Canada in 1924, although, as was most often the case, this may simply have identified the intended material.

34. The relevant passage from Poe's poem: "I stand amid the roar / of a surf tormented shore, / and I hold within my hand / Grains of the golden sand- / How few yet how they creep / Through my fingers to the deep, / . . . Is all that we see or seem / But a dream within a dream?"

   Loring took some liberties with Lamia, a female demon who was part serpent. Here, the dual nature of the figure is symbolized by the intertwining of the snake and the woman's hair.

35. They are not listed in the 1912–1913 New York City directory, and on a biographical data form for the Art Museum of Toronto, filled out by Frances Loring on

December 2, 1912, she gave her address at that time as 24 Adelaide Street, Toronto.

36. Sisler, *The Girls*, p. 22.

37. Edna Usher, "We're all in debt to these women," *The Telegram*, April 25, 1959, p. 29. It is true that the competition was tougher in the United States, where almost four hundred working sculptors were listed in the *American Art Annual* for 1909–1910.

38. Biographical information sheet submitted to the National Gallery of Canada in 1959.

39. An interview with Elspeth Chisholm for the CBC show *Profile*, first aired on July 22, 1956. My thanks to Ms Chisholm for sending me a copy of the programme notes.

FIGURE 8.
The studio of Frances Loring and Florence Wyle,
Church and Lombard streets, Toronto, 1914–
1920. Photographer unknown. Photo: gift
of the Estates of Frances Loring and Florence
Wyle, 1983.

14

two

EARLY PROFESSIONAL LIFE
IN TORONTO 1913–1920

What was the status of sculpture in Canada when Frances Loring and Florence Wyle first settled in this country? It should be noted that their work is being considered here in the context of academic sculpture produced in Canada at that time, with which it shared an intent: public monuments or fine art objects to be displayed for their aesthetic value. The history of this branch of sculpture is neither long nor prodigious compared to the long tradition of woodcarving in Quebec, which began late in the seventeenth century, or the carving practiced by the native peoples, notably the Inuit and Haida. These latter traditions, and their different purposes, whether decorative, ceremonial or commercial, form an integral part of our cultural heritage.

The status of academic sculpture in Canada around 1913 was better than it had been in the nineteenth century, largely as a result of riding on the coattails of its sister art, painting, and of general increased interest in the arts in Canada. An unprecedented amount of artistic activity in 1913 was marked by the publication that year of the first *Year Book of Canadian Art*, compiled by the Arts and Letters Club of Toronto. Nonetheless, it is telling that, while there were fourteen

essays devoted to painting in the book, and four to architecture, one brief article on the most noted sculptor of the day, Walter Allward, by Professor James Mavor, represented the art of sculpture in Canada.

Sculpture had always trailed behind the other arts in Canada. Hamilton MacCarthy, RCA (1846–1939), one of the more successful late-nineteenth-century sculptors, lamented the lack of encouragement given his profession in an article entitled "The Development of Sculpture in Canada" for *Canada: An Encyclopaedia of the Country*, published in 1898. He commented somewhat bitterly that "The chief interest of the Canadian *dilletante* centres around the fascinations of palette and brush, to the neglect of the finer subtleties of Form in the round." MacCarthy noted that while vast sums of money had been spent on painting, both native and foreign, sculptors of undoubted merit were being neglected, since it was a well-known fact that "good pictures are a better investment than real estate."[1] He also noted: "On visiting Toronto the traveller and lover of Art expresses surprise at seeing so few public monuments and so little Statuary in its public buildings, and this astonishment is not remarkable considering the size and importance of the Provincial

capital and its position as the seat of law and learning."[2]

Most English Canadians had had relatively little exposure to sculpture. MacCarthy pointed out that private patronage had been confined to the importation of copies of known classical subjects and to the work of some modern sculptors purchased by wealthy Canadians abroad. Some copies after European originals, belonging to local collectors such as J.M. Strachan and William Thomas, were shown at the first exhibition of the Toronto Society of Arts in 1847, alongside the architectural ornaments and the work of stone carvers that dominated the "Model Room," an innovation in Toronto at that time. With the proceeds of the first exhibition, plaster casts were purchased in New York for display in the second exhibition. It was hoped that the presence of copies of recognized historical masterpieces would elevate the state of the arts in this developing country. For this very reason, the chief superintendent of education, the Reverend Dr. Egerton Ryerson, travelled to Europe in 1856 to select a large number of reproductions, including plaster casts of antiquities, ancient and modern statuary, busts, etc. for the Educational Museum of Upper Canada. More than one

COLOUR PLATE NO. 1 *(Figure 46)*
Maurice Klein and Florence Wyle, *W.D. Young Memorial Fountain*, Kew Gardens, Toronto in 1987, showing replica of bronze baby by Frances Gage, installed in 1978. Photo by James Chambers.

thousand objects were procured and shipped to the museum, where they were chronologically arranged and catalogued. Gradually, portrait busts of distinguished Canadians were added to the collection, commissioned of the small band of available sculptors, which included Mildred Peel (the sister of Paul Peel, the painter), Hamilton MacCarthy, Frederick A. Turner Dunbar, Walter Allward, and others.

More than other professional artists, sculptors depended on commissions for their livelihoods. Considering the dearth of commissions in Canada in the nineteenth century, it is not surprising that so few sculptors chose to live and work here. The lack of a developed support system in the form of patrons, as well as the lack of foundries where the work could be cast, problems that lingered well into the twentieth century, led at least one sculptor, Louis-Philippe Hébert (1855–1917), to live abroad for long periods of time. Generally speaking, opportunities came in the form of private commissions for portraits and government commissions for public monuments. Works could also be sold through subscription, as was the case with a work by Samuel Gardner (1817–1893). A plaster cast of *Bust of Lord Metcalfe* had been shown at the Toronto Society of Arts first exhibition. A good deal of self-promotion was required, which might not always procure the sought-after commission. Hamilton MacCarthy wrote to the premier of Nova Scotia after learning of a proposed monument to the late Honorable Joseph Howe to offer his advice on public statues, and at the same time to request specifications. Perhaps he thought he would have a head start on other potential competitors with this information in hand,[3] but the commission went to another major figure working in Canada at

that time, Louis-Philippe Hébert.

It was not until 1900 that new names began to appear in the sculpture sections of the annual exhibitions held in Toronto at the Canadian National Exhibition (formerly the Dominion of Canada Industrial Exhibition and the Toronto Industrial Exhibition) and by the major art societies, the Ontario Society of Artists and the Royal Canadian Academy of Art. The turn of the century also saw an increased number of sculptors at the annual spring exhibitions of the Art Association of Montreal. These exhibitions were the only vehicle (apart from commissioned works) through which the sculptor could receive public exposure. Initially, sculpture was poorly represented, if at all. (For example, there was no sculpture exhibited at the Annual Exhibition of the OSA between the years 1891 and 1895 inclusive). Or sculptors were listed in the catalogues with architects, designers, or, even more inappropriately, with graphic artists. Recognizing the small encouragement of sculpture in Canada, the Royal Canadian Academy waived the annual membership fees due from sculptors from 1882 until 1905,[4] but it was slow to recognize the problems peculiar to sculptors. For instance, in their professional lives, the sculptor members were engaged primarily in the design of monuments; therefore, often they did not have smaller works available to send to the annual exhibitions. If they did not exhibit, they risked losing their standing with the Academy. In recognition of this, it was resolved by the council of the Royal Canadian Academy in 1910 that, in future, a photograph of an important work could be accepted in lieu of a statue or a model.[5] The OSA was even slower to recognize the particular concerns of sculptors, which cost them their most important sculptor members

in 1933, an event that will be returned to later.

The most important sculptor in Toronto around the time the Girls arrived was Walter Allward, who, according to James Mavor, writing in 1913, had "no competitor in Canada at the present time."[6] By 1913 he had completed an impressive number of commissions, including the memorial erected in Queen's Park to commemorate those who fell in the Northwest Rebellion of 1885 (1896), The War of 1812 Memorial in Portland Square (1906), several busts for the Normal School collection, and statues of Lieutenant-Governor John Graves Simcoe (1901), Sir Oliver Mowat (1905), and John Sandfield Macdonald (1909), all at Queen's Park. He was also responsible for the South African Memorial on University Avenue (1910). In 1913 he was working on three important commissions: the Bell Telephone Memorial, (Figure 7); the memorial to King Edward VII (which was to be erected at Ottawa but was never completed),[7] and the Baldwin-Lafontaine monument (1914) on Parliament Hill, Ottawa. His presence was certainly missed in a large showing of sculpture in Toronto in 1915, but the local press was quick to point out that his studies in recent years had been too large for exhibit in intimate exhibitions, and that "we are all aware how much he has done for Canadian sculptory."[8]

Allward, who had been born in Toronto in 1876, had been apprenticed to a local architectural firm, and later worked at a brickworks. He made a brief trip to England and France in 1899. The influence of Rodin, whose work he studied, is evident in many of his own works. Frances Loring held Allward in high regard, particularly the Vimy Memorial (1922–1936), which she used in her lectures in later years to illustrate the qualities she

FIGURE 18.
Walter R. Duff. *Miss Florence Wyle*, 1915. Drypoint etching, 27.65 x 17.45 cm (plate). National Gallery of Canada, Ottawa.

considered most essential in sculpture: dignity and repose.[9]

Frances Loring and Florence Wyle lost no time in integrating themselves into the local artistic community. Their earliest friends included Walter R. Duff (1879–1967), who etched Florence's portrait in 1915 (Figure 18); the painter Dorothy Stevens (1888–1966); and Robert Flaherty (1884–1951), photographer and filmmaker, who took many portraits of Loring and Wyle around 1919. (One of these images appears on the cover.) Initially Loring had a studio at 24 Adelaide Street, which Wyle seems to have shared late in 1912; then, in 1914, Wyle was listed in the Toronto directory at 114½ Church Street, the location of their studio (Figure 8, p. 14).[10] They began exhibiting immediately with the OSA, with whom Loring had shown in 1908, and Florence Wyle exhibited two works with the RCA for the first time in 1914. By June of that year, they had already established a name for themselves, being the subject (along with fellow sculptor Winnifred Kingsford, 1880–1947) of an article in *Women's Saturday Night* on "Women Sculptors in Toronto."[11] It was noted that "it is only within the last two years that women sculptors have been prominent," and that it was "gratifying to think that two talented young Americans should come to live amongst us." In 1917, Frances Loring became actively involved in the Women's Art Association of Canada; she was an artist member, organized a Sculpture Club, and staged an exhibition of her own work and Florence Wyle's that same year. Of the eighteen sculptors active in Toronto in 1915, seven were women.[12]

Nineteen-fifteen was a significant year for sculpture in Canada. The first exhibition devoted purely to sculpture was held at the the Art Museum of Toronto (known as the "Grange") from November 13 to December 15. Information about the exhibition is sketchy, but it appears that it was the idea of the director of the Art Museum, E.R. Greig. Loring and Wyle stole the show; more examples of their work were exhibited than of all the other sculptors combined.[13] The New York portraits they had done of each other, *Lamia*, the *Peacock Clock*, a Rodinesque piece entitled *Transmutation*, and *Dancing Boy*, were all included, as well as two recent heads, perhaps of the same model, which had not been shown previously. These heads, Loring's *The Old One* (Cat. No. 8) and Wyle's *Newsboy* (Cat. No. 9) allow for an interesting comparison in their styles. Wyle has considered the base to be quite independent of the head, an architectural element that serves to display the head to advantage, offering a clear definition of form and contour. Loring's more vigorously modelled head emerges from a base that has been considered an integral part of the design. This treatment was typical of Loring. A later example is the portrait of *Sir Frederick Banting* (Cat. No. 55).

The reviews were full of praise, and all registered surprise at the unexpected number of sculptors working in Toronto. The *Mail* critic wrote: "There is a popular impression abroad that the sculptors of Toronto . . . are of little weight. For that reason the exhibition of sculptory that may now be seen at the Grange is one of the most important so far arranged under the auspices of the Art Museum."[14] And these words appeared in the *Globe*: "It is not too much to say that the work of two young women who have recently come to the city has given a filip [sic] to sculpture here which it never previously possessed. These are Miss Florence Wyle and

Miss Frances Loring. Trained thoroughly in technique before they left their former home in the United States, they at the same time possess creative ability of a high order, and impart a richness and spirituality which moves the most casual observer."[15] Loring and Wyle may have had more involvement than just being exhibitors: in a letter to Eric Brown, the director of the National Gallery of Canada in Ottawa, Wyle wrote, "Miss Loring and I still hope that you may get down to our exhibition here at the Grange."[16] This exhibition may have given Sir Edmund Walker, president of the Art Museum and a champion of Canadian art, his first opportunity to view their work. He was to be instrumental in securing them a commission for the Canadian War Records Programme in 1918.

Commissions arising from the First World War were to provide sculptors with unprecedented opportunities to practice their art, but not in large numbers until the 1920s. In 1917 Frances Loring undertook a patriotic monumental group for the grounds of the Canadian National Exhibition, to be called *The Spirit of Canada*. Composed of staff (a mixture of plaster and straw), it featured an allegorical figure of Canada sending her sons to war (not unlike Allward's South African Memorial on University Avenue), flanked by an imperial lion and cubs, and was located just inside the Dufferin gates, the western

entrance to the grounds. It has not survived the Canadian climate, although it was still standing in 1925. A contemporary photograph in *Saturday Night* showed Frances Loring with her assistants, Winnifred Kingsford and Merle Foster, spattered with plaster and working at the surface of the male figure with an axe. It was erected in three weeks, and was well-received by the CNE Association since it "symbolized splendidly the Spartan like Canadian woman with her whole-hearted spirit of service and sacrifice."[17]

This was not the first time that Frances Loring had done work for the Canadian National Exhibition. She had modelled the 1915 CNE medal, awarded annually to the winners of the various competitions held at the Fair (Cat. No. 12). It had been designed by J.O. Orr, general manager of the CNE, inspired by an engraving in a book entitled *Angel's Island*, and was struck by P.W. Ellis and Company, a Toronto firm. The following year, Florence Wyle designed and modelled both the obverse and reverse of the 1916 medal, for which she was paid one hundred fifty dollars (Cat. No. 13). A delicate touch was required for these minute reliefs, which do not show to advantage in blown-up photographs. Also in 1916, both women exhibited in the Department of Fine Arts at the Ex; they appear in a photograph (Figure 19) taken at the CNE with their artist friends, Dorothy Stevens and Archibald Browne. They probably viewed the Exhibition of French and Belgian Art selected from the Panama-Pacific International Exposition in San Francisco in 1915, which had been shown in the spring of 1916 at the Albright Art Gallery in Buffalo and then secured for the CNE. The sculpture section contained an impressive selection of works by such respected figures as Albert Bartholomé, Emile Bour-

FIGURE 19.
At the 1916 CNE. Left to right: Pat Hardy, Dorothy Stevens, Frances Loring, Mrs. Archibald Browne, Archibald Browne, Florence Wyle. Photographer unknown. Photo: gift of the Estates of Frances Loring and Florence Wyle, 1983.

FIGURE 20.
Frances Loring and Margaret Scobie. *Miss Canada*, outside Eaton's main store, 1917. Staff, location unknown. Courtesy of the Archives, Eaton's of Canada Limited.

COLOUR PLATE NO. 2 *(Cat. No. 50)*
Florence Wyle, *Study of a Girl*, c. 1931. Painted
plaster, H. 135.5 cm. Art Gallery of Ontario,
Toronto. Gift of the Estates of Frances Loring
and Florence Wyle, 1983.

delle, M-J-A Mercié, and Auguste Rodin.

Nor was *The Spirit of Canada* Frances Loring's first monumental work done in Canada. Earlier in 1917, along with fellow sculptor Margaret Scobie, she had erected a twelve-foot figure, called *Miss Canada*, over the north door of Eaton's then main department store on Yonge Street (Figure 20). This figure was also staunchly patriotic, "standing in an attitude of triumph . . . holding proudly up the ensign of Canada in her right hand while in the left, posed on the pedestal, is a shield of all the Canadian Provincial arms." She was crowned with laurels and maple leaves "à la Canadienne."[18] The two women had only one week to create the sculpture, which was also made of staff, and they worked under a make-shift tent in a yard at the corner of Louisa and Teraulay Streets (Figure 21). It was erected on June 20, in good time to celebrate the fiftieth anniversary of Confederation, for which it had been intended; ironically, an American had erected a monument to symbolize Canada's nationhood.

In September 1918, Eric Brown wrote to Frances Loring on behalf of Sir Edmund Walker, who was chairman of the board of trustees of the National Gallery and a member of the War Memorial Funds committee, to ask whether she and Florence Wyle would be interested in creating several bronze figures, based on "the various types of girl war workers," for the Canadian War Records. It had been on the initiative of Sir Max Aitken, an expatriate Canadian who had become a member of the British House of Commons and had been appointed officer in charge of War Records, that a committee was organized in 1917 to compile a record of the Canadian war effort. Soon after its initiation, Sir Edmund Walker told Sir Max (who became Lord Beaverbrook in 1918) that the war

effort in Canada was not being recorded, nor had Canadian artists been asked to contribute to the scheme.[19] Walker was put in charge of the work to be done in Canada and Brown was helping him.

Eric Brown wrote, "When I was at the Toronto exhibition I saw the various types of the girl war workers in their working clothes, munition makers, aeroplane girls, land workers, fruit pickers etc, and it struck me that they were very fine subjects for a series of small bronzes . . . I can imagine you have seen the girls I mean yourself, and have thought of them in terms of bronze and therefore the idea is not new to you."[20] He asked Frances to consider the subjects she would choose and their most appropriate size. He also asked if Wyle, who had been a patient at the Gravenhurst Sanitarium from 1917 to 1918 because she was suffering from respiratory

FIGURE 22.
Florence Wyle. *Memorial to Nurse Edith Cavell,* 1919–1921. Bronze relief, H. 213.0 cm. On the grounds of Toronto General Hospital, Toronto, Ontario. Photo by James Chambers.

FIGURE 23.
Frances Loring. *The Mercer Memorial,* 1921. Bronze relief, H. 155.4 cm. Moss Park Armouries, Toronto. Photographer unknown. Photo: gift of the Estates of Frances Loring and Florence Wyle, 1983.

problems, would be able to work on the project as well.

The response was immediate and highly positive. The women had spoken between themselves of the war work being done by their painter colleagues, and had hoped that there was similar work a sculptor could do.[21] They agreed that women workers would translate well into bronze, and began working on sketches right away, planning first to go through some of the munitions plants to select the best subjects. Precedents in this area had been set by the Belgian sculptor Constantin Meunier (1831–1905) and the French Jules Dalou (1838–1902), representatives of the Realist movement in sculpture, who typically chose workers as their subjects. Some American sculptors had also turned their attention to the theme of the worker, among them Mahonri Young, Abastenia St. Leger Eberle, and Chester Beach.[22] In Canada, Marc-Aurèle de Foy Suzor-Côté (1869–1937) and Alfred Laliberté treated genre subjects that included the worker. Loring and Wyle were formally commissioned to do the work on September 18, 1918, and each was advanced the sum of one hundred fifty dollars that November.

By late October the women had toured the plants and the War Record work was well under way; having had more time to reflect upon the possibilities of the subject, Wyle suggested they represent some of the male workers as well ("they were so wonderfully sculptural") and do some relief work, since they felt it was "practically impossible to do the girls at the machines in any other way."[23] Loring did two reliefs,[24] but only one, *Noon Hour at a Munitions Plant* (Cat. No. 21), was cast. Sometime in March, 1919, the first seven figures, including *Noon Hour* (Cat. No. 19) and *Furnace Girl* (Cat. No. 20), referred to in correspondence as "the Groover," were sent to the New York factory of the Gorham Manufacturing Company to be cast in bronze. The remaining figures would be done by a Canadian company, William A. Rogers Limited, in Toronto, perhaps because time was limited, and because it may have been less costly to have the work done locally. They do not seem to have had much faith in the local foundries, however, and Wyle's *Farm Girl* (Cat. No. 18) was used as a test piece.[25]

Eric Brown wanted all the work completed by September in time for a special exhibit of the Canadian part of the war memorials to be held at the Art Gallery of Toronto from October 18 to November 12, 1919.[26] Although the catalogue listed all their works, a total of sixteen, as being in bronze, only seven, those cast at Gorham, were ready in time for the Toronto showing. The work at Rogers dragged on because of labour troubles, illness, and lack of coal, and two of the bronzes were still unfinished in June 1920. Even when all the work was done, payment by the War Memorial Funds Committee was slow, and the Girls had to borrow money to pay the foundry while writing letters to Eric Brown, pleading for final payment. (Their funds were depleted because they bought a property in the country in 1919 and an old frame church, to use as a home and studio, in 1920.)

The figures were very well received. Barker Fairley wrote that, to many people, they were the most interesting thing in the War

FIGURE 24.
Frances Loring. *Sketch for a war memorial*, c. 1925. Plaster model, location unknown. Photo by Pringle and Booth Ltd. Photo: gift of the Estates of Frances Loring and Florence Wyle, 1983.

Records exhibition, and that "the dress and attitude of women workers in field and factory, from being the subject of 'farmerette' jokes, has here been turned to account as the source of a beauty that is finely nervous and supple."[27] And in a letter to Florence Wyle, Eric Brown relayed the fact that A.Y. Jackson was tremendously taken with them: "He says you have done a series of bronzes which make him wish to knock down all the statues in Toronto and let you replace them with anything you wish."[28]

Similarity in subject matter for this commission again invites a comparison of their respective contributions. All of Loring's figures, like *Furnace Girl*, are actively engaged in their task, while half of Wyle's have been caught in a moment of rest, and more than one has taken up the classical *contrapposto* pose, with the weight carried fully on one leg, and the tilt of the shoulders counterbalancing that of the hips, as in *Farm Girl*. Florence would turn again to the theme of the worker pausing for refreshment around 1938 with *The Harvester* (Cat. No. 64). Both women have used the folds in the workers' garments to enliven the surface and underline the action being performed, to the point where the uniforms seem drenched, revealing the underlying anatomy. Florence's surfaces are more detailed, having been broken up by

COLOUR PLATE NO. 3 *(Cat. No. 55, Figure 53)*
Frances Loring, *Sir Frederick Banting*, c. 1934.
Bronze, H. 62.5 cm. Art Gallery of Ontario,
Toronto. Gift of the Estates of Frances Loring
and Florence Wyle, 1983.

a system of meaningful lines and creases. Frances has paid less attention to detail; the surfaces are broader, less broken up by folds, which are used more to describe lines of force.

Late in the summer of 1919, Frances Loring was working on a frieze entitled *Noon Hour in a Munitions Plant* (Cat. No. 21), a large relief. Wyle had probably also begun modelling her *Memorial to Nurse Edith Cavell*, another large relief (Figure 22), which occupies its original site, at the south-east corner of College Street and University Avenue, on the grounds of the Toronto General Hospital. The large scale of these works made a larger working space necessary, and Loring and Wyle consequently bought some land at Cherrywood, on Kingston Road, east of Toronto, which they used as a summer studio. Wyle had been given the commission for the Edith Cavell Memorial, probably in the spring of 1919; she had submitted a small model earlier that year, which had been inspected by the hospital trustees, then approved by Sir Edmund Walker in March. Jules F. Wegman, an architect, was responsible for designing the architectural framework

for the bronze relief, which was erected in late August 1921, apparently without ceremony.[29]

As Loring did in her frieze, Wyle has generalized the action in her relief, so that it does not recall a specific scene, but instead "symbolized the ideals for which the nursing profession stood with relation to war service."[30] In both works, the figures are bent forward, conveying their sense of duty in spite of extreme fatigue. Loring used the walking figure in profile again in the *Mercer Memorial* (Figure 23), unveiled in 1921 by the Prime Minister of Canada, the Right Honorable Mr. Arthur Meighen, at the old City Armories, which once stood on University Avenue. (This bronze relief is now located in the Moss Park Armories, on Queen Street East, Toronto.) In her workers' frieze, and in its later adaptation to a war-memorial sketch of the industrial workers who had made victory possible (Figure 24), the figures are dressed in contemporary work clothes. By contrast, the Mercer figure is robed in ancient Greek dress and carries the attribute of honour or victory, a laurel wreath. She is

not tied to a specific time, place, or event, but, as the personification of an abstract concept, takes on a grander, more universal meaning.

Monuments erected in memory of the Great War represent one of the main categories of activity in which sculptors, particularly Frances Loring, would be engaged in the 1920s. Several themes and motifs that first appeared in the significant work done by Loring and Wyle for the Canadian War Records would be taken up again later on in their careers. The bronze war workers are representative of their finest work from that period, which was fast drawing to a close; they are among the last works done in a realist vein. The world changed rapidly after the Great War ended, and the sculpture of the Girls reflects the era in which it was produced. While the Girls remained faithful to their academic training, firmly maintaining their belief that a solid understanding of the human figure and anatomy were the basis of sculpture, their work over the next twenty-five years bears the unmistakable imprint of the advancing tide of modernism.

ENDNOTES

1. Hamilton MacCarthy, "The Development of Sculpture in Canada," *Canada: An Encyclopaedia of the Country*, Vol. 4, ed. J. Castell Hopkins (Toronto: The Linscott Publishing Company, 1898), p. 372.

2. MacCarthy, p. 378.

3. Letter to the Honorable David Murray, Premier of Nova Scotia, from Hamilton MacCarthy, RCA, dated March 21, 1903. Public Archives of Nova Scotia, Halifax.

4. Minutes of the council meeting of the Royal Canadian Academy, April 13, 1882, p. 27, rescinded in minutes of the council meeting, May 13, 1905, p. 143. Royal Canadian Academy Papers, Public Archives of Canada, Ottawa.

5. Minutes of the council meeting of the Royal Canadian Academy, November 25, 1910, p. 169. Royal Canadian Academy Papers, Public Archives of Canada, Ottawa. The resolution was prompted by the resignation of Walter Allward, a valuable associate member of the academy, who specialized in monumental sculpture. He was persuaded to stay and became a full academician of the RCA in 1914.

6. James Mavor, "Walter Allward, Sculptor," *The Year Book of Canadian Art 1913* (Toronto: J.M. Dent, 1913), p. 253.

7. The figures of Truth and Justice were cast in bronze; then the war put a halt to the project. They were taken out of storage in the recent past and placed before the Supreme Court Building in Ottawa.

8. "Local Artists show Sculptory," *Mail*, November 27, 1915.

9. Frances Loring gave many public lectures during her lifetime in her crusade to promote the art of sculpture in Canada. Sometimes the contents of these talks were summarized in the press. In February 1934, in an address to the Women's Art Association, she included Allward along with Michelangelo, Epstein, Meunier, Mestrovic, and Rodin as great sculptors of their day. In later talks, she spoke of the qualities she admired most about Allward's work, and contrasted it to the "cheap melodrama" of the Canadian War Memorial in Ottawa by the March family from England (Toronto *Star*, April 11, 1946).

10. An article in the Toronto *Star* (November 16, 1912) refers to both of them living in a studio at Adelaide and Victoria Streets. Wyle may have used this as her mailing address when she sent work from the United States to Canada for exhibition, since she lists this address in the exhibition catalogues while continuing to live in the United States. In any case, it is not clear exactly when she became a permanent resident of Toronto.

11. Estelle M. Kerr, "Women Sculptors in Toronto," *Women's Saturday Night* (June 20, 1914), p. 25.

12. According to a list contained in the 1915 Sculpture Exhibition file in the Art Gallery of Ontario Archives. The seven included: Winnifred Kingsford, Bessie Muntz, Beverley Robinson, Lady G.W. Ross (Mildred Peel), Mabel M. Stoodley, Frances Loring, and Florence Wyle.

13. The other exhibitors—J. Lisney Banks, Frederick Coates, Emanuel Hahn, Alfred Howell, Winnifred Kingsford, Edgar Laur, and Marcel Olis—showed a total of twenty-one works; the Girls together showed forty-one.

14. "Local Artists show sculptory: splendid exhibition is now on view at the Grange," *Mail*, November 27, 1915.

15. "Toronto Sculptors spring a surprise," *Globe*, November 15, 1915.

16. Letter from Florence Wyle to Eric Brown, December 2, 1915. Curatorial file, *Dancing Boy*, National Gallery of Canada, Ottawa.

17. Canadian National Exhibition Association, *Report and Financial Statement for 1917*, delivered at the thirty-ninth annual meeting, p. 36.

18. "Miss Canada in Yonge St.: Heroic Figure of Lady of Confederation in Front of T. Eaton Co. Store," *Globe*, June 20, 1917.

19. R.F. Wodehouse, *Check List of the War Collections* (Ottawa: The National Gallery of Canada, 1968), pp. 3–4.

20. Letter from Eric Brown to Frances Loring, September 10, 1918. National Gallery of Canada Archives, file 5.42 Loring.

21. Letter from Frances Loring to Eric Brown, September 15, 1918. National Gallery of Canada Archives, file 5.42 Loring.

22. See Frank Owen Payne, "The Tribute of American Sculpture to Labor," *Art and Archaeology*, Vol. 6, No. 2 (August, 1917), pp. 82–93, which cites the rise of the American labour party as the reason for the increasing interest in this theme.

23. Letter from Florence Wyle to Eric Brown, October 25, 1918. National Gallery Archives File 5.42 Wyle.

24. Loring also did a relief called *The Grinder*, which was exhibited in the 1919 War Records exhibition held at the Art Gallery of Toronto, but only the plaster is known to exist today. (Collection of the Art Gallery of Ontario. Gift of the Estates of Frances Loring and Florence Wyle, 1983. 83/44.)

25. All the pieces cast by Rogers but two—Florence's *Farm Girl* and *Moulder*—are in poor condition today, their surfaces peeling. It may be that the percentage of iron

in the metal was too high. By 1922, Loring noticed that the surface of *The Oiler* (also cast by Rogers) was peeling and requested that it be sent back to the foundry for refinishing. (Undated letter from Loring to Eric Brown, National Gallery of Canada Archives 5.42-L Canadian War Artists.)

26. *Catalogue of Pictures, Sculpture, Drawings, Etchings and Lithographs done by Canadian Artists in Canada under the authority of the Canadian War Memorials Fund and exhibited for the first time at the Art Gallery of Toronto.* It was noted in the prefatory note that "the Canadian section is still as incomplete as the overseas section . . ." as not all the work had been completed and gathered together by November, 1919.

27. Barker Fairley, "At the Art Gallery," *The Rebel*, Vol. 4, No. 3, December, 1919, p. 124. My thanks to Robert Stacey for pointing this article out to me.

28. Letter from Eric Brown to Florence Wyle, November 3, 1919. National Gallery of Canada Archives 5.42 W.

29. This information was provided by Jules Wegman to M.O. Hammond, who recorded it in his notes on Canadian monuments, now in the Archives of Ontario. The money for the memorial was contributed largely by Ontario schoolchildren (*Globe*, August 25, 1921). By December 11, 1918, the Edith Cavell Memorial Fund had raised $4,000, and the trustees of the hospital were ready to consider models for a memorial, according to the Toronto General Hospital board of trustees minutes (p. 47). By February 12, they had been invited to inspect a small model (minutes, p. 61), and consulted Sir Edmund Walker, who gave his full support to Florence Wyle (minutes, March 12, 1919, p. 65).

30. "Can't get very far without hard work," *Star Weekly*, August 27, 1921.

COLOUR PLATE No. 4 *(Cat. No. 67)*
Frances Loring, *Eskimo Mother and Child*,
c. 1938. Painted plaster, H. 190.0 cm. Art
Gallery of Ontario, Toronto. Gift of the Estates
of Frances Loring and Florence Wyle, 1983.

three

THE SALON OF TORONTO'S
ART WORLD 1920–1948

The period following the First World War through the Second represents the height of the artistic careers of Frances Loring and Florence Wyle. It began when they moved to a new studio, a building that had housed the Sunday School of Christ Church, Deer Park. It had once stood at the corner of Yonge Street and Lawton Boulevard, but had been moved, around 1910, across the Vale of Avoca to its present site east of Mount Pleasant Road (Figure 25; Figure 26, p. ii). A basement was dug under the house; plumbing was installed, and a colossal fireplace was built in the south wall. The building's capacious interior was ideally suited to the needs of two sculptors who would soon be working on large-scale monuments, architectural reliefs, and fountain figures.[1] In addition to being their studio, the building, known as "the church," was the official head office of the Sculptors' Society of Canada for many years, and was the gathering place for Toronto's artistic community until a new generation of artists came on the scene after the Second World War.

Regarded as highly unconventional by the general populus at the time, and often living close to the poverty line, especially during the Depression, the Girls nonetheless were highly regarded as artists and attracted a richly varied and interesting group of friends. Included were academics such as professors Herbert Davis and Robert MacIver, brother of Keith MacIver, the Girls' closest friend. Keith MacIver was involved in mining operations in northern Ontario with Frances Loring's father, but spent his winters in Toronto. Musicians Evelyn Pamphilon, Jeanne Dusseau, Gwendolyn Williams, and John Goss, and other artists, including their good friend A.Y. Jackson, (Cat. No. 44), were early visitors to the Church, as was Fred Varley (Cat. No. 22). Florence sculpted portraits of many of their friends over the years, so the studio must have gradually taken on the appearance of a "Who's Who" of noteworthy personalities of the 1920s and 1930s. Of the Group of Seven, she did a head of Lawren Harris (Cat. No. 43), and hoped to do one of Arthur Lismer, but it was never done. Patrons and supporters of the arts, such as the Elys (Cat. Nos. 23, 27, and 28) and the Honorable Vincent Massey, Canadian Minister to the United States from 1926 to 1930 and High Commissioner in London from 1935 to 1946, were also represented. The anarchist Emma Goldman, who also numbered among their friends, was a visitor to Canada from November 1926 to February 1928, in exile from the United States. In Toronto, Goldman was helped by the Girls, who arranged for her to give a special drama course at Hygiene Hall,[2] in Elm Street.

In the early twenties, it was said that Loring and Wyle were two of the most important sculptors in Canada, and Eric Brown wrote that the several examples of their work possessed by the National Gallery were "looked upon as among the most brilliant of the Canadian sculpture."[3] At the annual meeting of the OSA, in the spring of 1920, they were elected members of the society in spite of the fact that neither had submitted work to the annual exhibition that year; the rules regarding election were suspended because Loring and Wyle were considered "artists of reputation."[4] Actively involved in the OSA, Loring and Wyle were elected to the hanging committees (Figure 27), and to the executive council on more than one occasion. Loring was a member of the council from 1922 to 1926, Wyle in 1929. Wyle was a constant contributor to the annual exhibitions until all the sculptor members of the society resigned in 1933.

In addition to the OSA, Loring and Wyle were involved in the RCA; they exhibited

FIGURE 25.
Exterior south elevation of the studio before 1952. Photo by Herb Nott. Photo: gift of the Estates of Frances Loring and Florence Wyle, 1983.

FIGURE 27.
The OSA Hanging Committee, 1928. From left: Gustav Hahn, F.H. Bridgen, L.A.C. Panton, Florence Wyle, H.S. Palmer, T.W. Mitchell, Wyly Grier. Photo by M.O. Hammond. Province of Ontario Archives, Toronto.

with the academy for a number of years before they were elected associate members in November, 1920. Wyle became an academician in 1938—the first woman sculptor to do so—and Loring in 1947. They also continued their membership in the Women's Art Association of Canada. Loring was a vice-president from 1930 to 1934, chairman in 1935 and 1936, and president from 1938 to 1940. Wyle was the only woman on the jury of selection—she represented the sculptors—for the British Empire Exhibition held at Wembley in 1924 and 1925, and Loring sat as an adjudicator for the Willingdon Fine Arts Competition in 1930.

Throughout the years, both artists raised active voices on matters pertaining to the arts. Loring was the more vocal of the two. She frequently lectured, usually on the history of sculpture.[5] On one occasion she drew up and circulated a petition in support of Eric Brown during the National Gallery controversy in 1932. Brown had been attacked by a group of conservative painters who accused him of prejudice in the acquisition of works of art for the National Gallery's collection. Wyle's advice to these artists "to leave amateur politics alone and paint" was the subject of a column in the *Mail* on December 10, 1932. In the late 1940s, when a local

manufacturer erected a water tower in the vicinity of Loring's Queen Elizabeth Monument, which at the time marked the eastern entrance to the Queen Elizabeth Way (Figure 28, Pl. No. 5), Loring launched protests through the OSA (to which she had been reinstated in 1948) and the SSC. She claimed that the authorities had failed to take the necessary precautions to prevent the defacement of the view of this monument by factory buildings. The monument, designed by Loring and W.L. Somerville, was comprised of a stylized lion, at the base of a tall pillar surmounted by a crown. Wyle was responsible for the profile relief of the Royal couple at the base of the pillar. The monument was moved to Gzowski Park, on Lakeshore Boulevard West, in 1974 to allow for the widening of the highway (Figure 29).

As a member of the Continuation Committee of the first Conference of Canadian Artists held in Kingston, Ontario in 1941, and of the Federation of Canadian Artists (FCA), which resulted from it, Frances Loring worked to achieve the professed objects of the FCA, one of which was to promote public and government support for the visual arts, particularly during the war. She wished to discourage the point of view that art was an extravagance during wartime; she had raised this issue at the Kingston conference. A petition was drawn up by the Montreal Committee of the FCA in 1942 urging the federal government to enlist the talents of Canadian artists. A copy of the petition could be signed at the studio of Loring and Wyle. When the umbrella organization, the Canadian Arts Council (CAC), was set up in 1945, Loring was representative for the Sculptors' Society of Canada, one of the sixteen national arts societies that comprised the council.

Just as their public activity differed, so their artistic careers were quite separate during these years. Frances Loring devoted herself primarily, though not exclusively, to war memorials and architectural sculpture, while, generally speaking, Florence Wyle preferred to work on a more modest scale, designing fountains for private gardens and undertaking portraits and figure work. Figure work was Wyle's preference, for she felt it was better sculpture,[6] and much of her work was not intended to serve a practical purpose. During the 1920s, when the country was in need of a large number of war memorials to commemorate the Great War, both Loring and Wyle, along with most other Canadian sculptors, rose to meet the demand. For a brief period, the sculptor was needed and his or her talents were recognized.

WAR MEMORIALS

Most of the war memorials in Canada today were erected after the First World War.[7] Their numbers, size, and character reflect the unprecedented scale of the conflict and the huge loss of human life involved. Before the Great War, the energetic figure of a soldier engaged in some activity related to battle, and sometimes accompanied by a female personification of Victory, served to commemorate the patriotism and heroism of those who fell. Such are the memorials that were designed by Hamilton MacCarthy (Halifax, Brantford, and Ottawa) and George Hill (London, Ontario), for example, in memory of the two hundred fifty Canadians who were killed in the Boer War (1899–1902). The First World War (1914–1918) took the lives of more than sixty thousand Canadians.

The plucky figures of the Boer War memorials were inadequate to convey the enorm-

ity of Canada's loss, and sculptors turned instead to allegorical figures, which were capable of embodying more universal concepts. Walter Allward, in particular, favoured the use of allegory, not only in his colossal Vimy Memorial, but also in the Stratford War Memorial (1922) which has two Rodinesque figures, "Spiritual Triumph" and "Brute Force," and the Peterborough War Memorial (1929), which also has two figures, "Humanity" and "Aggression." Alternatively, the introspective figure of a solitary uniformed soldier, complete with his weapons, like a saint or martyr with his attributes, stands to represent his fallen comrades. Frances Loring's St. Stephen War Memorial (Figure 30), unveiled in 1926, and an identical monument with minor changes cast in 1929 for Augusta, Maine, are characteristic of this new spirit. Loring's work is strikingly similar to Emanuel Hahn's Fort William Memorial (Figure 31), unveiled in 1921, of which many copies were made and scattered across the eastern part of the country.[8]

In anticipation of the hundreds of war memorials that would be erected in the next decade, the Ontario Advisory Committee on War Memorials was formed in 1919,

FIGURE 28.
Frances Loring and W.L. Somerville. *The Queen Elizabeth Monument*, 1939–1940. Indiana Limestone, H. 362.4 cm, in its original location at the eastern entrance to the Queen Elizabeth Way. Photo by Jean Gainfort Merrill. Photo: gift of the Estates of Frances Loring and Florence Wyle, 1983.

FIGURE 29.
Frances Loring. Detail of *The Queen Elizabeth Monument* in its new location, 1987. Photo by James Chambers. See Pl. No. 5.

COLOUR PLATE NO. 5 *(Figures 28 and 29)*
Frances Loring and W.L. Somerville,
The Queen Elizabeth Monument in its present
location in Sir Casimir Gzowski Park, Lakeshore
Boulevard West, Toronto. Photo by James
Chambers.

chaired by George A. Reid, principal of the Ontario College of Art, and comprised of representatives of the OSA, the Society of Graphic Art, and the Ontario Association of Architects. None of the representatives was a sculptor. A circular was published to advise those interested in erecting war memorials, and it contained suggestions as to their treatment, a list of conditions affecting their promotion and erection, and suggestions as to type, which included fountains, symbolic groups, public buildings, mural paintings, and so on.

The committee was ineffectual, however, partly because of the lack of publicity, and it disbanded by the fall of 1922. Out of a concern to stem the tide of bad monuments being erected across the country by inexperienced citizens; and to encourage the involvement of professional sculptors and limit the

involvement of the commercial monument companies, Frances Loring suggested the formation of an alternative organization. It would be national in scope, and composed of disinterested individuals, including representatives of the RCA, the Society of Architects, perhaps the director of the National Gallery, and a "newspaper man for publicity purposes." The organization should act in a purely advisory capacity—suggest suitable locations, provide referrals to those best suited to do the work, or act as judges in competitions.[9] It does not appear that such a committee was ever established. However, Loring carried on her crusade as convenor of the War Memorial Committee within the OSA and tried to enlist the help of the Royal Architectural Institute of Canada in setting up a conference to discuss improving the conditions in war-memorial competitions early in 1928.[10]

It is likely that the Girls were working on war memorials as early as the summer of 1919.[11] A number of models exist in photographs, but it is unknown for which specific project they were intended. (See, for example, Figure 24.) Loring and Wyle may have entered the Canadian Battlefields Memorials Competition, which was announced in the fall of 1920, the intention of which was to erect landmarks on the eight battlefields of France and Belgium where the Canadian Corps accomplished its most notable achievements. Walter Allward's entry was chosen for Vimy Ridge. In 1923 the Girls were the only women among eight sculptors to submit designs for the Sault Ste. Marie War Memorial. The competition was won by Alfred Howell; the memorial was unveiled in 1924.

Again, both Loring and Wyle submitted models for the National Commemorative War Monument competition in 1925. The

FIGURE 30.
Frances Loring. Clay model for the *St. Stephen War Memorial*, c. 1925. Dimensions unknown. Photo by Pringle and Booth Ltd. Photo: gift of the Estates of Frances Loring and Florence Wyle, 1983.

FIGURE 31.
Emanuel Hahn. *Fort William War Memorial*, c. 1921. Stone, dimensions unknown. Photographer unknown. Photo (retouched): Special Collections, E.P. Taylor Reference Library, Art Gallery of Ontario.

FIGURE 32.
Florence Wyle. *Sketch for a war memorial,*
c. 1925. Plaster, dimensions unknown. Photographer unknown. Photo: gift of the Estates of
Frances Loring and Florence Wyle, 1983.

federal government had decided in 1922 to
erect a memorial in Ottawa. There would
be a two-stage competition open to all architects, artists, and sculptors resident in the
British Empire, and to British subjects by birth
who were resident elsewhere. In consultation
with Eric Brown, the general conditions of the
competition were drawn up, and a public
notice inviting designs was issued in February
1925. The specifications concerning the final
form were loosely defined. It was stated
that the monument was to be "expressive of
the feelings of the Canadian people as a
whole, to the memory of those who participated in the Great War and lost their lives in
the service of humanity."[12] The first stage
involved designs drawn on paper, from which
the finalists were chosen and asked to submit
plaster models made to the scale of one inch
to the foot. Another interesting specification, in light of the increasing collaboration
between sculptors and architects in the
1920s and 1930s, was that, should the designer
be an architect, he or she would be required
to associate with a sculptor approved by the
assessors, and vice versa. This followed the

example set earlier by the Canadian Battlefields
Competition.

The small, two-figure grouping included
in the exhibition (Figure 32, Cat. No. 30) was
probably Florence Wyle's entry. The figures
were to be life-size and symbolize "Canada,
mourning, sending her son forth to battle for
the Right and arming him with the Sword
of Righteousness and the Shield of Faith." It
is placed atop a high plinth. Wyle had not
collaborated with an architect, and perhaps as
a result of this, the figural and architectural
elements are not successfully combined. Loring, on the other hand, welcomed the challenge of integrating disparate elements on a
monumental scale, and her entry (see Figures
33 and 34), submitted with the architect
W.L. Somerville, was one of the seven selected for the second stage of the competition.[13] As in many of her designs for
monuments in this period, Loring's major
allegorical figures appear to emerge from the
wall against which they are set. Here, however, they have not simply been sculpted in
high relief, but are in three-quarter round.
By carrying the relief concept (which, by nature, integrates the figure with the wall) to
its furthest limits, she has created a truly
monumental work, the over-life-size figures
gaining strength from the stone framework
(Figure 35, p. xiv). We have the maquette
for one of the side groupings, representing the
sacrifice made by the mothers (Cat. No. 31).
If Loring were following the rules governing
scale, these would have been more than nine
feet high.

Loring and Somerville did not win the
commission, which was awarded instead to the
English sculptor Vernon March for his design, the "Great Response." Loring disliked
the monument, which she later described
as "cheap melodrama." However, she did not

abandon her design, but resubmitted it to the competition for the Galt War Memorial, again with William Somerville, in 1928. Probably because of the lack of funds, the original design had to be pared down, to eliminate the side groupings. This left the single figure of "Victory" on one face, and that of "Peace" on the other, which is how it appeared on its unveiling in 1930 (Figure 36) and has remained to this day.

A single allegorical figure characterizes another major war-memorial commission, which came Loring's way in the late 1920s. It was ordered by the Law Society of Upper Canada for the library at Osgoode Hall. (See Figures 37 and 38.) Inspired by the Rupert Brooke poem "These laid the world away," the seven-foot marble figure depicts a young man casting off the robes of daily life in the service of humanity. He stands before a marble panel inscribed with the names of the Law Society members who lost their lives in the Great War. Wyle used the same quotation as the heading of a memorial plaque designed for Northern Secondary School at the end of the Second World War (Figure 39). In its posture, which symbolizes the act of self-sacrifice, Loring's figure bears a strong resemblance to Rodin's Jean de Fiennes, which forms part of the *Burghers of Calais*. This cel-

ebrates the six men who offered their lives for their city during the Hundred Years' War in 1347.

One of Loring's two sketches (Cat. No. 33) for the memorial was accepted, and she signed a contract on September 15, 1926. It was very specific in describing what was expected in terms of the design, including the deadline date of January 1, 1928.[14] A second contract, dated January 31, 1928, was made when Loring failed to complete the work by the specified date. She went to Italy the following summer to select the marble and supervise its cutting, since it was too costly to bring back the uncut block, and "impossible to find a first class marble cutter in Canada."[15]

The monument was completed in time for an unveiling on November 10, 1928, by the lieutenant-governor of Ontario, at which Frances Loring was not present. The whole affair made the unique problems faced by the sculptor painfully clear. Bronze sculpture could be brought into Canada free of duty, but marbles executed abroad from models made in Canada were not exempt from tax. The sculptor stood to lose any profit she might have made from the commission.

Apart from the problem of obtaining the marble, and contracting technicians to cut it, one of the main reasons for Loring's failure

FIGURE 33.
Frances Loring and W.L. Somerville. One side of a model for a war memorial featuring the figure of Victory, 1925. Plaster, location unknown. Photo by Pringle and Booth Ltd. Photo: gift of the Estates of Frances Loring and Florence Wyle, 1983.

FIGURE 34.
Other side of Figure 33, featuring the figure of Peace. Photo by Pringle and Booth Ltd. Photo: gift of the Estates of Frances Loring and Florence Wyle, 1983.

Colour Plate No. 6 (*Cat. No. 75*)
Frances Loring, *Dawn*, c. 1948. Painted plaster,
100.7 × 142.5 cm. Art Gallery of Ontario,
Toronto. Gift of the Estates of Frances Loring
and Florence Wyle, 1983.

to honour her contract with the Law Society was the fact that she had taken on a great deal at one time. During the fall of 1927 she agreed to model a central group of three figures and a tympanum figure panel for the memorial chamber of the Parliament Buildings in Ottawa (Figure 40).[16] She probably had to drop everything to take on this project, since the dedication ceremony for the chamber took place on July 13, 1928. Also in 1927, she was working on a memorial tablet to Dr. Alpheus Todd, former librarian of Parliament (Figure 41).[17] Florence Wyle had been left to arrange for the patination of the Todd memorial, which was cast in May 1928, while Loring was in Italy working on the Osgoode Hall memorial.

For the central group of three figures, Loring returned to the theme of the sacrifice of the mothers, which had been one of the side groupings in her 1925 National War Memorial entry (Cat. No. 34). *The War Widow* is elongated, well-suited to her location high up on a finial; her head is turned to one side as though she is caught in a pensive moment. Accompanied by two children, she would not be confused with the Virgin Mary; indeed, she is closer to traditional representa-tions of Christian Charity. Both the widow and the high relief of the *Recording Angel*, in the tympanum below her, are compatible with the neo-Gothic style of the architectural programme. (They were simplified and boldly stylized so as to be easily read from below.) The same bold stylization, evident in the flattened tubular clouds, for example, was applied to reliefs Loring made for the interior of the Bank of Montreal, executed in 1948 (Cat. No. 75, Pl. No. 6). The commission for the *Recording Angel*, drawn from the imagina-tion and executed on a monumental scale, allowed Loring to give full expression to her talents as a designer; in its design consciousness (note the symmetrical inward-pointing wings of the flanking angels), it is typical of the Art Deco style that prevailed at the time.

RESPONSE TO MODERNISM

It is obvious from her architectural designs, which required a certain amount of stylization, that Frances Loring was sensitive to prevail-ing artistic trends, but her response to the advent of modernism was not nearly as marked as that of Florence Wyle. From around 1926, Florence Wyle's style evolved from a realism characterized by carefully articulated surfaces and an anatomical accuracy almost mannered in its detail, to an increasingly stylized treatment of the human form. A gradual distillation occurred in her art, so that the more abstract components were empha-sized at the expense of detail. By 1943 she felt that the best sculptors of her day were those who had "learned to accent and simplify, to balance one form against another, to study light and shade and drawing—in a word to know that sculpture is harmony of mass, as music is harmony of sound, and that only the fundamental ideals and aspirations of the

FIGURE 36.
Frances Loring and W.L. Somerville. *The Galt War Memorial*, c. 1930. The photograph has been inscribed with ink to indicate desired changes to the steps. Photographer unknown. Photo: gift of the Estates of Frances Loring and Florence Wyle, 1983.

FIGURE 37.
Frances Loring. *The Osgoode Hall War Memorial* Great Library, Law Society of Upper Canada, Osgoode Hall, Toronto, 1928. Marble, 213.2 cm. Photo by James Chambers.

FIGURE 38.
Detail of Figure 37. Photo by James Chambers.

FIGURE 39.
Florence Wyle. Northern Secondary School *War Memorial Tablet*, Northern Secondary School, Toronto, c. 1946. Stone. Photo by Nott and Merrill. Photo: gift of the Estates of Frances Loring and Florence Wyle, 1983.

human race have the enduring quality necessary for translation into stone."[18] While she was never able to carry the distillation process as far as a Brancusi, for instance, she kept apace with the modernism of her less radical contemporaries in North America and abroad.[19]

Florence Wyle moved to a more modern means of expression largely because of an increased exposure to contemporary modern sculpture. She made a trip abroad, to France, Belgium and England, for purposes of "study and travel" in 1924. However, this trip does not appear to have had any immediate impact on her work. She may have known of the sculptors Bourdelle, Maillol, Mestrovic, and Manship, all "conservative moderns,"[20] before her trip; but it was not until around 1926, when she probably saw a number of modern sculpture exhibitions, held principally at the Art Gallery of Toronto, that her work begins to show their influence around that time.

The main reason for the increasing frequency of these exhibitions was the introduction of a sculpture court,[21] dedicated to Sir Edmund Walker, in the newly expanded Art Gallery of Toronto in 1926. The Art Gallery was able to properly accommodate sculpture exhibitions of its own works or of works borrowed from sister institutions in Canada and the United States. Local sculptors encouraged the exhibition committee of the Gallery to bring in the exhibitions they wanted to see. Emanuel Hahn wrote to the Art Gallery on behalf of the sculptor members of the OSA in 1926, requesting the Bourdelle exhibition, which had been organized by the Carnegie Institute in Pittsburgh.

Significant early exhibitions included "Sculpture and drawings by Aristide Maillol" (June 22 to August 31, 1926); "A selected

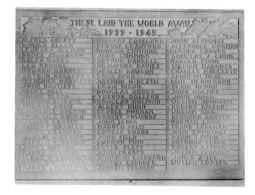

group of European sculpture" (organized by A.C. Goodyear for the Albright Art Gallery in Buffalo and shown in Toronto in December 1927), which included the work of Frank Dobson, Jacob Epstein, Herman Haller, Georg Kolbe, Aristide Maillol, Ivan Mestrovic, and Carl Milles; and "Sculpture by Paul Manship" (April 14 to May 6, 1928). In 1928, a significant number of pieces of modern sculpture were purchased for the permanent collection, including Mestrovic's *Mother at Prayer* (Figure 42).[22] The influence of Mestrovic's wood reliefs is evident in Wyle's late *Young Worker* (Cat. No. 96).

Evidently, then, North American audiences were aware of contemporary European sculpture and had a propensity for its more conservative strain. The modernism of these sculptors often manifested itself in a conscious archaizing or primitivizing, in which forms were simplified and articulated by a decorative overlay of line. Without exception, the sculptors kept the human figure as their subject. In 1928, the Toronto critic Augustus Bridle commented that the work of Canadian sculptors demonstrated a "...fine balance between progressiveness and traditional reserve, without flamboyant radicalism."[23] While Europeans, during this period, were returning

to the use of the figure, which they treated with a new classical solidity following a period of pure abstraction, Canadians had never abandoned it. They never participated in Cubism or other radical movements in sculpture before or during the First World War. Even the work of the more conservative strain of European sculptors would likely have struck Canadian sculptors as progressive.

Notable among the books once in the Girls' possession that indicate their interest in contemporary sculpture are Maurice Denis's 1925 publication on Aristide Maillol, in French, and Stanley Casson's *Twentieth Century Sculptors*, published in 1930. Exactly when the Girls acquired these books is not known. However, there is evidence that they were around the studio in the mid-thirties. Frances Loring's *Sea Horse Fountain*, of about 1938 (Figure 43), is a paraphrase of Paul Manship's *Dancer and Gazelles* (Corcoran Gallery, Washington), which was exhibited at the Manship exhibition at the Art Gallery of Toronto ten years earlier, and is illustrated in Casson's 1930 publication.

Also illustrated are two torsos, one by Alexander Archipenko, the other by John Skeaping. One of the main practitioners of the partial figure was Aristide Maillol (Figure 44), and several of his torsos were included in an exhibition of his work at the Art Gallery of Toronto in 1926. Commentators on Maillol, including Denis, have pointed out his preference for describing the "architecture of the body," before concerning himself with the details. As Albert Elsen has stated, the absence of limbs simplified for Maillol the problem of "composing" a figure and gave him more succinctly the decorative or overall largeness of effect. As the female figure fulfilled his ideal of the essential, Maillol generally favoured the female torso.[24] The Girls' colleague Elizabeth Wyn Wood first showed a *Torso* at the first SSC exhibition in 1928.

Florence Wyle, who stated that the female is "Mother of the Race," and in fact used this as the title of one of her major pieces around 1930 (Cat. No. 48), also felt that the female torso permitted her the fullest possible expression sculpturally. It was through her treatment of the female torso that Wyle's evolution towards modernism was effected. One of her first partial figures was the small *Study of a Girl* (Cat. No. 32), exhibited at the OSA Annual Exhibition in 1926. The innovations present in this small piece are amplified in the larger *Study of a Girl* (Cat. No. 50), evidently done several years later, using the smaller version as a model. In contrast to an earlier female nude, *Sunworshipper* (Cat. No. 14), which strikes a dramatic pose, *Study of a Girl* is in repose and incomplete, having being severed at mid-thigh.

COLOUR PLATE NO. 7
Florence Wyle in the studio, c. 1950. Photographer unknown. Photo: gift of the Estates of Frances Loring and Florence Wyle, 1983.

The surface of the figure has been smoothed out and simplified so that individual anatomical features are not articulated. This has affected the anatomical accuracy of the figure: the arms have been unnaturally lengthened, to create a smooth, unbroken line, which curves down and across the lower part of the body, connected with the hand tucked behind a piece of drapery. All the anatomical details have been suppressed in favour of the design, except the backbone, which has been accentuated to emphasize the serpentine curve of the back.

The complete figures of the *Young Mother* (c. 1928; Cat. No. 45) and *Birdbath* (c. 1935; Cat. No. 58) also display a strong concentration on line and contour. Nothing interferes with the outline of the graceful *contrapposto* pose of the mother in the first work. Detail, particularly in the hair, has a linear quality, as it does in the birdbath, where the girl's

stylized curls are echoed in the Greek-scroll motif encircling the bowl. The clear outlines, simplified forms, and linear detail also characterize the work of Paul Manship, who was featured at the Art Gallery of Toronto in 1928.[25] His archaizing tendency appealed to the contemporary taste for earlier, more stylized forms of art. Emanuel Hahn and his wife, Elizabeth Wyn Wood, were deeply interested in Egyptian art at that time.[26]

The torso became a constant theme in Florence Wyle's work beginning in 1930 with the monumental *Torso* (Cat. No. 48). Wyle also called the piece *Mother of the Race*. Inspired by contemporary moderns and in emulation of the ancient Greeks whom she so admired, the torso was an ideal subject for her. It predominates until the end of her career in a variety of media. *Mother of the Race* is significant for a number of reasons. It was her first true torso. (Before, she had made truncated figures.) Also, she carved the stone herself because she was making the piece for the trustees of the National Gallery of Canada, who could not afford to pay her asking price, two thousand dollars.[27] Wyle was requested to reduce it. She did, but only reluctantly, since the two thousand dollars would not cover the cost of the materials or a good marble cutter.[28] She commented: "But artists must sell to go on producing—though we could do far more and better work if we were not always cramped by lack of money." The piece was purchased by the National Gallery in 1933. Eric Brown felt it was ". . . quite one of the most outstanding things of its kind done so far in Canada."[29] But once again, it was at the sculptor's expense.

Over the years, Wyle's torsos became increasingly stylized and "artified"; the stumps of limbs were "trued" so that they no longer hinted at accidental breakage. Whereas in

FIGURE 42.
Ivan Mestrovic. *Mother at Prayer*, 1926. Marble, H. 119.4 cm. Art Gallery of Ontario, Toronto. Gift of Mrs. Timothy Eaton, 1928.

FIGURE 43.
Frances Loring and *Sea Horse Fountain*, c. 1938. Photo by Herb Nott. Photo: gift of the Estates of Frances Loring and Florence Wyle, 1983.

41

FIGURE 44.
Aristide Maillol. *Torso for Ile de France*, 1921.
Bronze, H. 120.0 cm. Art Gallery of Ontario,
Toronto. Courtesy of American Friends of Canada Committee. Gift of Peter D. Meltzer, in
memory of the late David and Elise Meltzer,
1983.

Mother of the Race, the arms appear to have
been broken off, the deliberate elimination of
the arms of the Winnipeg Art Gallery's small
wooden *Torso* (Cat. No. 59) is obvious,
given that the artist has deliberately smoothed
the terminating points. *Draped Torso* (c. 1939;
Cat. No. 70); the National Gallery's draped
wooden *Nude* (c. 1944, Cat. No. 73); and
a later work, *Sea and Shore* (c. 1950; Cat.
No. 80) have also been treated in this manner.
The degree of stylization was greatest when
she worked in wood because of the nature of
the material and her desire to exploit the
grain to the fullest. This is evident to some
extent in *Nude*, and is more obvious in the
later Rivers series of 1949 (Cat. Nos. 77 and
78), where the result is somewhat mannered.

Wood became a popular material during
the thirties. It was far less expensive than
marble, and more workable on a smaller scale;
attractive, saleable items could be made
speculatively in wood or in ceramic form with
less serious financial consequences to the
artist if the piece did not sell immediately. In
a review of the 57th Annual Exhibition of
the RCA in 1936, it was noted that there was
a gradual increase in the use of wood.[30] For
their diploma pieces for the Royal Canadian
Academy, Loring used butternut wood and
Wyle used mahogany (Cat. Nos. 61 and 76).
Around 1942, Loring wrote a pamphlet for
servicemen entitled "How to get started: Wood
carving for pleasure." (It was published by
the YMCA War Services and the Canadian
Legion Educational Services.)

Working in wood encouraged a greater
variety of textural effects, especially when the
sculptor allowed the chisel marks to remain
in the wood. Wyle used this technique in
a piece called *Head*, in white wood, exhibited
in the 1935 Sculptors' Society show, and
illustrated in the catalogue. Her interest in

texture spilled into other media, and may
have influenced her approach to modelling in
clay. In the late 1930s, she began applying
a stippled finish to the surface of her figures;
one example is the head of Charles Goldhamer (Cat. No. 62). She was not alone in
these experiments: Elizabeth Wyn Wood
was using similar textural effects around that
time, for example in *Woman with Skein*
c. 1935, (Estate of Elizabeth Wyn Wood and
Emanuel Hahn). Sensuous, textured surfaces

of thick impasto emerge in many contemporary paintings, partly influenced by German Expressionism.

The problems particular to their art became increasingly apparent to sculptors during the 1920s, through their involvement with the various war-memorial projects and the government. The constant obstacles they encountered, and the failure of the major exhibiting societies to meet their special needs, prompted the sculptors to consolidate their energies and form the Sculptors' Society of Canada in 1928. Sculpture was enjoying a higher profile in Canada than ever before; the sculptors must have felt the time was right to attempt to better their situation.

THE SCULPTORS' SOCIETY OF CANADA

Dear Sir/ We wish, hereby, to resign from the Ontario Society of Artists. This move is prompted by no ill will. . . . Realizing, however, that our contributions and our needs are different from those of the majority, and since we are united as a body, we feel that our withdrawal is in the best interests both of the Ontario Society of Artists and of ourselves as Sculptors. We consider that our energies should be devoted more specially to the furtherance of sculpture, but you may count upon our cooperation, should the need arise at any time."[31]

The letter was dated February 8, 1933 and signed by Emanuel Hahn, Florence Wyle, Elizabeth Wyn Wood, and Frances Loring. In accepting their resignation, the society expressed its regret that "sufficient justice had not been possible to be given to sculpture on account of inadequate facilities for its exhibition." The sculptors had tried to effect some

changes in the treatment of sculpture within the OSA; for example, they had requested that sufficient space be reserved in the galleries to accommodate sculpture, that no pieces be placed in corridors and the passages between rooms, and that, if no sculptor member had been elected to the hanging committee, one should be brought in to act in an advisory capacity when the sculpture was being judged. They also recommended that the sculpture be judged at the beginning of the selection procedure.

These four individuals, with Quebec sculptor Henri Hébert, whom Loring and Hahn had visited in Montreal to interest him in the idea, had formed the Sculptors' Society of Canada in the summer of 1928. The letters patent incorporating the SSC were sent to Frances Loring on September 16, 1932. The reason for the delay had to do with a disagreement between the Federal Government and the Society over the proposed charter fee. Loring claimed it was too high for so small an organization to carry, unduly burdening each member. The fee was probably reduced, since Loring wrote to Ottawa, grateful that the Secretary of State was able to grant them a charter "without so great an outlet of money." (August 20, 1932, SSC Papers, Public Archives of Canada, Ottawa). There are no formal records of the society before 1933. Loring was a major force in the society from its inception; without her, it may still have been born, but would have been considerably weaker. She served as secretary-treasurer from 1928 to 1942 (because, as she said, she spoke French and owned a typewriter); she was vice president in 1942 and 1950; and was president from 1944 to 1946 and again in 1949. In 1960 she was voted "special lifetime advisor to the society." Florence Wyle served as vice president in 1938

and as president in 1942, but she was much less active in the society's affairs than Loring.

Loring regarded the activities of the society as "largely educational and of great benefit to the country."[32] Its object, as stated in its constitution, was three-fold: to promote closer cooperation amongst the sculptors of Canada and the encouragement, improvement, and cultivation of the art of sculpture; to hold exhibitions and lectures in the principal cities of Canada and elsewhere; and to act in an advisory capacity for the erection of public memorials. These objects were almost identical to those of the National Sculpture Society in the United States, which was incorporated in 1896, and with which Frances Loring must have been familiar.

The SSC went a long way towards achieving its objectives. First, it united sculptors, mostly from Ontario and Quebec, in its ranks. Loring and Wyle welcomed the first Eskimo sculptor to membership in 1960. The society vetted any issues that would affect the professional work and status of sculptors; for example, when a sculptor was not included on the panel of judges in the design competition for a new Canadian five-cent coin in 1950. As well, it organized a large number of exhibitions. The first was held at the Art Gallery of Toronto from October 6 to November 1, 1928 (Figure 45). Like at the first sculpture show in 1915, the Girls dominated. The same exhibition was installed in slightly altered form at the National Gallery of Canada in Ottawa in 1929, where a second SSC exhibition was held two years later. In June 1935, Frances Loring, secretary of the SSC, wrote to Eric Brown proposing that the National Gallery place an exhibition of the SSC in its circuit of travelling shows.[33] A travelling exhibition was subsequently organized and shown in Ottawa, Montreal, Winnipeg, Ed-

COLOUR PLATE NO. 8 (*Cat. No. 83*)
Florence Wyle, *Spring*, c. 1951. Sumac,
H. 35.9 cm. Mr. Jennings Young, Toronto.

monton, Vancouver, and Calgary in 1936 and 1937. Other travelling exhibitions were proposed during the 1940s, and the SSC sent a show of photographs to Germany in 1948. (It was a more practical solution to send the pictures than the works themselves.) The society also collaborated with the National Gallery in 1939 to send an exhibition of work to the New York World's Fair. Florence Wyle was represented by five pieces, including *Study of a Girl* (Cat. No. 50), the *Cellist* (Cat. No. 61), and *Draped Torso* (Cat. No. 70); Frances Loring sent four pieces: *Eskimo Mother* (Cat. No. 67, Pl. No. 4), *Sir Frederick Banting* (Cat. No. 55), *Miner* (Cat. No. 60), and *Girl with Fish* (Cat. No. 53). On July 15, 1939, *Saturday Night* devoted a full page to a photo story entitled "Canadian Art makes its first bow in the US" to mark the occasion.

The Girls also submitted entries to the Metropolitan Life Insurance Company's sculpture competition in 1938, as did Elizabeth Wyn Wood, Alfred Laliberté, and Allan Cameron (1905–1938). The piece would be exhibited at the Fair. Four elongated Graecian figures (Cat. No. 63) represent one of Florence Wyle's interpretations of the prescribed theme: a group symbolic of "the average American family consisting of not less than three persons—mother, father, and

child." New York sculptor Thomas Lo Medico was the winner, selected from 257 entries, for his pneumatic-looking group of three figures. Wyle's entry was in step with the stylized figures of other entrants such as William Zorach, who had been invited to compete.

In addition to heightening the profile of sculpture in this country, the Sculptors' Society of Canada worked towards improving the professional practice of sculpture in Canada. In 1946, Frances Loring, who often spoke for the society, proposed writing a pamphlet, a guide to how to buy a public monument. Later, around 1957, she worked on a booklet to be published by the society as a guideline for fellow sculptors on available supplies and services. It was also to include samples of contract forms, and an approximate scale of prices. By 1952, the SSC had had revisions made to the customs regulations that broadened the definition of sculpture so that works cast in materials other than bronze could be brought in to Canada duty-free.

Loring thought sculptors should be involved in the decoration of public buildings—not surprising, given her preference for architectural work. Throughout the 1920s, sculptors collaborated with architects and landscape architects on many war-memorial projects; in the late thirties, they again worked together. Loring's letter to the minister of public works at the height of the Depression in 1935, to inquire whether there was any provision for sculptural work in the government's building programme, was almost a plea: "We need scarcely point out that these are difficult times for sculptors, particularly in Canada, and we venture to suggest that any work of this nature which could be commissioned from Canadian Artist-Sculptors would be of great cultural encouragement."[34] The minister replied that the building project's

FIGURE 45.
First exhibition of the Sculptors' Society of Canada, 1928, Art Gallery of Toronto. Photographer unknown. Photo: gift of the Estates of Frances Loring and Florence Wyle, 1983.

contractor would decide, but the sculptors recognized that contractors would usually take the least expensive route. In 1960 the SSC was still trying to ensure that two per cent of building funds go towards sculptural decoration, and they were supported in this by the RCA and the Royal Architectural Institute of Canada (RAIC).

SCULPTURE AND ARCHITECTURE

In a critical essay that examined sculpture in Canada from 1938 to 1948, Elizabeth Wyn Wood notes that the period had shown "an almost complete reversal of emphasis and patronage" from previous years; in 1948, the most vigorous Canadian sculpture was to be found either on buildings or in parks, or in private homes.[35] She said the 1930s had been dominated by "Salon Sculpture." The bulk of the work produced had been shown in galleries, which subsequently bought some pieces, but which had since "unconsciously rejected" the art of sculpture.

Loring and Wyle certainly fitted into the pattern; the type of work they produced depended on who was paying. It ranged in size from large-scale reliefs for architectural settings to small domestic-scale pieces. Throughout the thirties and forties, both women continued to exhibit with the major societies (except the OSA) and were included in a four-woman show at the Art Gallery of Toronto in 1942, with Jacobine Jones (1898–1976) and Dora Wechsler (1897–1953). They also showed work in an exhibition entitled "Sculpture in the Home," selected by the SSC and held at Eaton's Fine Art Galleries in mid-April, 1946. It was a milestone exhibition, for it demonstrated the change in emphasis from the previous years. By showing smaller works in a commercial

space (this was the second time the SSC had held an exhibition at Eaton's), they hoped to attract a broader audience for sculpture.[36] Wyle exhibited her *Cellist* (Cat. No. 61) and a terra-cotta version of the small *Torso* (Cat. No. 59), and Loring showed *Girl with Fish* (Cat. No. 53).

Their execution of sculpture for architectural settings began early in the 1920s. Frances Loring, in addition to her collaboration with William Somerville in the war-memorials competition, and with John Pearson in the Memorial Chamber, was involved, with Florence Wyle, in the decoration of several Toronto churches. In 1923, both executed painted-plaster reliefs displaying the symbols of the Evangelists for the spandrels of the Byzantine dome of St. Anne's Church. The decorative programme of the church was supervised by J.E.H. MacDonald, of the Group of Seven; Fred Varley and Frank Carmichael were also involved. The *Madonna and Child* relief (Cat. No. 25) was probably made around the same time as the reliefs for St. Anne's. In 1922, Loring had modelled a life-size figure of Christ, crowned and dressed in a girdled alb to symbolize kingship, for St. Mary Magdalene's Church on Ulster Street in Toronto. It was part of a rood, designed by William Rae, who was also the designer of an altar for Bishop Bethune College, in Oshawa. Florence Wyle designed the four plaster angel candlestick holders decorating the Rae altar, which was included in the first exhibition of Architecture and the Allied Arts. This highly successful exhibition was held at the Art Gallery of Toronto from February 11 to 27, 1927, under the auspices of the Ontario Association of Architects. The principal organizers were a group of architects known as the "Diet Kitchen School," and included W.L. Somerville and John M. Lyle.

The Girls exhibited with The Allied Arts on more than one occasion; the shows became biannual events from 1927 until 1939. Over the years, Loring showed her models for the War Memorial Competition (1927), a photograph of the Osgoode Hall War Memorial (1929), and the model for the Galt War Memorial (1931); Florence Wyle showed her stylized Art Deco relief, *The Cellist* (Cat. No. 61) in 1933, a shield for the Canadian Bank of Commerce, and the *Deer Panel*, made for Baron Byng High School[37] (Cat. No. 46) in the 1931 exhibition. On one occasion, she exhibited the model of the drum for the Gage Memorial Fountain in Hamilton, designed by John Lyle. The drum, which is decorated with the figures of dancing children in relief, is a typical Beaux-Arts treatment of objects such as decorative urns, and a theme to which Florence Wyle was unquestionably well-suited. The theme was suggested by Jane Gage, who was erecting the fountain in memory of her parents.

Frances Loring undertook several fountain designs, notably *Girl with Squirrel* (c. 1922) for the grounds of Parkwood, Colonel Sam McLaughlin's home in Oshawa; *Mermaid Fountain* (c. 1923) (of which Cat. No. 26 is a cast of the head); *Girl with Fish* (Cat. No. 53); and *Sea Horse Fountain* (c. 1938; Figure 43). She also wrote an article for the magazine *Canadian Art* on the subject of garden sculpture.[38] But fountains were an area in which Florence Wyle excelled. It will be recalled that her first major works executed at the Art Institute of Chicago were for fountains, and that one of her first commissions was for a drinking fountain (Cat. No. 1)—a sculpture in high relief, which was nonetheless entirely functional. In 1920, she designed a "fountain baby," as well as the portrait reliefs for the W.D. Young

Memorial Fountain (Figure 46, Pl. No. 1) in Kew Beach Gardens, Toronto. Sir John Eaton sat on the advisory committee for this memorial; it was for the Eaton estate in King City that Wyle later modelled two fountain figures, *Dancing Baby* (c. 1928; Figure 3), and *Child with Flute* (c. 1929), both of which were cast in bronze.[39]

The "cult of the fountain" was noted in a lengthy article, "Nymphs and Fauns as Magic Fountains in Canadian Gardens," written by Katherine Hale and published in the *Star Weekly* magazine on August 11, 1923. When building resumed after the war, and with the country's increased prosperity, home owners turned their attention to beautifying their properties. High-spirited figures such as children, fauns, and nymphs were considered to be appropriate subjects for fountains, and these could be complemented by water crea-

tures, such as frogs (Cat. No. 47) or turtles (Cat. No. 84).[40] Wyle happily incorporated children into her fountain projects, for example *Baby Fountain* (c. 1928; Cat. No. 42) and *Baby with Dolphin* (c. 1923; Cat. No. 29). The motif of a child riding a dolphin had a long tradition in fountains; Wyle's former teacher, Lorado Taft, had incorporated just such a motif in his *Fountain of the Great Lakes* (c. 1903); it is a tradition that stretches back to Renaissance times.

Sculptors found valuable colleagues in landscape architects like the Dunington-Grubbs. Two years after lecturing on the subject of garden sculpture at the Women's Art Association, Frances Loring and Lorrie Alfreda Dunington-Grubb, also a member of the association, organized a three-day sculpture exhibition on the grounds of the WAA as the annual summer entertainment. Lorrie-Alfreda Dunington-Grubb was one of the Canadian sculptors' most fervent supporters. She and her husband, Howard, employed them in their business. As well, Dunington-Grubb had written an article called "Sculpture as Garden Decoration" (*Canadian Homes and Gardens*, March, 1927). She wrote: "It is difficult to obtain good garden ornaments in this country and all encouragement possible should be given to those of our Canadian artists who are trying to popularize this form of art." Wyle probably received the commission for the *Bain Fountain* (Cat. No. 72; Figure 47) for H.R. Bain through the Dunington-Grubbs, who were responsible for landscaping the Bain home in north Toronto.

As for collaborating with architects, it has already been mentioned that Florence Wyle designed the drum for a fountain by John Lyle. One important contribution Lyle made to sculpture was his crusade for what he called "A Canadian Architecture." (In

FIGURE 46.
Maurice Klein and Florence Wyle. *W.D. Young Memorial Fountain*, 1920, Kew Gardens, Toronto. Relief portraits and original bronze figure by Florence Wyle. The original figure was stolen soon after its installation. Photo: gift of the Estates of Frances Loring and Florence Wyle, 1983. See Pl. No. 1.

FIGURE 47.
Florence Wyle. *Bain Fountain*. Photo by Herb
Nott. Photo: gift of the Estates of Frances
Loring and Florence Wyle, 1983.

FIGURE 48.
View through the Harry Oakes Pavillion, Niagara
Falls, Ontario, featuring *Orioles* and *Blue Jay*,
reliefs by Florence Wyle, c. 1938. Photo by James
Chambers.

1931, his article entitled "Canadian Ornament
goes Native" was published in the *American
Architect*.[41]) As it turned out, the crusade
primarily involved the application of Canadian
motifs to the buildings he designed. With
its profile heightened, architectural sculpture,
and particularly sculpture on Canadian
themes, saw increased application in the 1930s
and 1940s. A 1938 editorial in the *Journal
of the Royal Architectural Institute of Canada*
states that, despite themselves, "for the first
time in Canada architects' conversation is
likely to turn to the subject of sculpture on
building."[42]

One major project in which Loring and
Wyle were engaged was in Niagara Falls,
Ontario. The architect responsible was W.L.
Somerville, who had worked with Frances
Loring on the Galt War Memorial, and for
whose new addition to St. Michael's Hospital
in Toronto she had modelled the figure of
St. Michael. (It still occupies its niche over
the Bond Street entrance to the hospital.)
Loring and Wyle were first commissioned to

model a series of reliefs of native birds for
the Harry Oakes Pavillion (Figure 48) in the
Oakes Garden Theatre at Niagara Falls in
1938. Wyle did four—*Seagulls, Bluejays, Wrens*,
and *Orioles* (Cat. No. 66)—and Loring
three—*Pigeons* (Cat. No. 65), *Canada Goose*,
and *Owl*. Soon after, they undertook a series
of reliefs for the Canadian approach plaza
to the Rainbow Bridge, which included a
garden, a service station, and a bus stop.
North Country (Cat. No. 71), *Rainbow* and
Farm by Florence Wyle decorate one of the
garden walls, while a number of reliefs of
wild flowers were placed over the shops of the
arcade. The relief *Johnny Canuck and Uncle
Sam* was also done by Wyle. Loring executed
several larger-scale reliefs—*The Invention of
the Wheel* and *Deer Panel*—as well as smaller
panels on an industrial theme.

Loring and Wyle collaborated on the
Canadian coat of arms for the Customs House.
The Rainbow Bridge project provided the
Girls with income in financially troubled times,
but Frances Loring commented that their
work was being ". . . sneaked in sort of as
construction work" because "they [the gov-
ernment] are so scared that the opposition
should realize that art is being indulged in

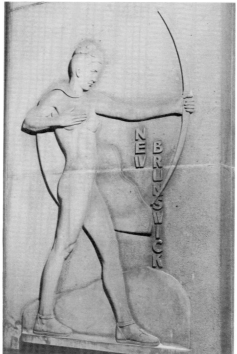

FIGURE 49.
Frances Loring. Relief panel *Ontario* for the Bank of Montreal, after 1948. Stone. Photo by Gilbert Milne. Photo: gift of the Estates of Frances Loring and Florence Wyle, 1983.

FIGURE 50.
Florence Wyle. Relief panel *New Brunswick* for the Bank of Montreal, after 1948. Stone. Photo by Gilbert Milne. Photo: gift of the Estates of Frances Loring and Florence Wyle, 1983.

during war times."[43] As we have seen, she was completely averse to this attitude. Pearl McCarthy, art writer for the *Globe and Mail*, praised the Rainbow Bridge project highly, and perhaps to help ward off any criticism, she wrote: "In this case of the Rainbow Bridge, the very best that could be desired has been procured at minimum cost, with the result that the people of Canada actually own what costs each citizen a smaller fraction of a cent . . . . We own inspiring art for ourselves and coming Canadians. That is good business, good art, and good pride for Canada."[44] The sculpted reliefs do not have a great impact today, however, since they are scattered and have been obscured by structural additions or vines.

The 1946 commission for twelve reveal panels for the new Bank of Montreal Building at the corner of King and Bay streets in Toronto also specified Canadian content. F.H. Marani, of the architectural firm Marani and Morris, in consultation with W.S. Allward, decided, with the six sculptors sharing the work (Loring, Wyle, Hahn, Wyn Wood, Jacobine Jones, and Donald Stewart), that the "Spirit of the Provinces," with the main pursuits of the people, be represented. The gender of the figures on either side of each door was also specified; for instance, flanking the central door of the King Street facade was the male figure of Ontario, with his attributes symbolic of industry, science, and the arts; opposite him, also by Frances Loring, was the female personification of Quebec, whose spool and lyre represent the province's

FIGURE 51.

Elizabeth Wyn Wood. *Reef and Rainbow*,
1927–1930. Cast tin on black marble base,
24.8 x 95.9 x 25.2 cm. Art Gallery of Ontario,
Toronto. Gift from the Albert H. Robson
Memorial Subscription Fund, 1950.

CANADIAN SCULPTURE

Canadian sculptors were slower than their
painter colleagues to express a national spirit
in their art. Elizabeth Wyn Wood, twenty
years younger than the Girls, was the first to
attempt in sculpted form what the Group
of Seven had achieved in painting; that is,
to interpret the Canadian landscape in a
modern idiom. This was much more difficult
to do in three dimensional form than on a
flat canvas, where colour and illusion aid the
artist; but Wyn Wood successfully combined
relief work with sculpture in the round to
achieve the desired effect, as in *Passing Rain*,
first shown at the 1928 SSC exhibition at
the Art Gallery of Toronto (now at the
National Gallery of Canada in Ottawa), and
in *Reef and Rainbow* (1927–1930; Figure 51).
Her innovative work was a breath of fresh
air.

textile industry and folk-music tradition. The
sculptors selected their own subjects (Figures
49 and 50). Florence Wyle chose New
Brunswick and Prince Edward Island, both of
which were to be female. Wyle commented
at the time that it was "too bad to have to
please a committee but we get paid for it."[45]
The female allegory *Dawn* (Cat. No. 75)
was one of Loring's reliefs for the interior of
the bank, and was apparently accompanied
by a male panel, *Dusk*.[46]

The exterior sculpture was criticized, at
the time, for its incongruity with the modern
building of which it was a part. The problem: the apparent weight of the relief fastened
to the wall denied its character as a "screen,"
which is how the wall is presented in modern
architectural practice.[47] While the figures
have been adapted to their situation as part
of the "ironed-out" wall, they are still substantial figures, which seem to stand before
the wall rather than be a part of it. Also,
they were awkward to view, placed high above
the heads of passers-by. On the positive side,
when the bank finally opened its doors in
1949, Pearl McCarthy, ever supportive of
Canadian art, commented that Canadian art
history had been made with this building,
which had been designed by Canadian architects and decorated by Canadian sculptors
using Canadian themes.

The strong Canadian element present in
the work of Loring and Wyle was typically
expressed through the human figure rather
than the landscape. On the occasion of
a retrospective of their work at the London
Public Library and Art Museum in 1962, one
writer perceptively noted that the exhibition
was "a review of 50 years of a nation that
went to war twice, that has miners, Indians,
Eskimoes [sic], refugees from other countries,
and a nation in which men and women have
fought for science and for an art of their
own."[49] More than just a neat summary of the
contents of the show, these words describe
the significance of the work. Both women felt
that good sculpture must be honest, and
that "the best art is an expression of the life
around you; you must do the things you
know."[50]

Subjects derived from native-Canadian
arts first entered Florence Wyle's work in 1927,

when she was asked by anthropologist Marius Barbeau to travel to Hazelton, Kispiox, Kitwanga, Hagwilgel, and nearby places in British Columbia to record in sculpted form the totem poles that were in rapidly deteriorating condition. She asked her painter friend Anne Savage (Cat. No. 41) to join her. The work would be shown in an exhibition of West Coast art at the National Gallery of Canada in November and December, 1927, and would be composed of "the most artistically interesting examples of this Indian craft work procurable and to include with it as much as is possible of the best work done by our modern Canadian artists in the same region."[51] Wyle showed six plaster totem poles and three in iron, which were, perhaps, the book-ends or paperweights (Cat. Nos. 36 to 38) inspired by the totem imagery. Book-ends, paperweights, and lamp stands, of which Cat. No. 35 may have been the wooden

prototype, were made in large number, undoubtedly with an eye to commercial distribution, like the candlesticks Wyle had made in 1912 (Cat. No. 6). In fact, candlesticks, totems, and small iron owls were available for purchase at the Grange craft shop in December, 1929.[52]

A stylized interpretation of the owl decorates the frame of the superbly modelled *Indian Mother and Child* (Cat. No. 39). Its incorporation into the surrounding border alludes to the carved decoration of native dwellings; along with the slightly protruding "sill", it turns the frame into a window through which the group is viewed. By making the frame into an architectural element, Wyle has created an environment for her subjects. The relief is given greater meaning because the viewer is situated within that same environment.

Around 1938, Frances Loring did her interpretation of a native mother and her child, the monumental *Eskimo Mother and Child* (Cat. No. 67), of which she was particularly fond. Like Wyle, Loring chose a typical scene of mother and child. She was inspired by a photograph (Figure 52) taken by the topographer, J.R. Cox in 1916. It had appeared in a number of publications where Loring possibly saw it, including the American publication *Art and Archaeology* (Vol. 20, No. 2, 1925), Diamond Jenness's *The People of the Twilight* (New York: MacMillan, 1928), or the Rev. C.E. Whittaker's *Arctic Eskimo: A Record of Fifty Years Experience and Observation among the Eskimo* (London: Seeley, Service and Co., 1937).[53] Loring may also have had access to it through Dr. Jenness himself, an ethnologist at the National Museum of Man (now the Canadian Museum of Civilization) in Ottawa. The use of aboriginal people as subject matter was

FIGURE 52.
"Manigurin and her baby Itayuk, in coat hood," May 1916. Photo by J.R. Cox. Reproduced in *Art and Archaeology*, Vol. 20, No. 2 (1925), p. 78. Photo (copy): Royal Ontario Museum, Toronto.

FIGURE 53.
Frances Loring with *Sir Frederick Banting*, c. 1950. Original photo by Everett Roseborough. Photo: gift of the Estates of Frances Loring and Florence Wyle, 1983. See Pl. No. 3.

not new to Canadian sculpture: Canadian Art Club member A. Phimster Proctor had modelled Indian heads and the figures of warriors in the first decade of the twentieth century, and other examples include Alfred Laliberté's *Jeunes Indiens Chassant* (c. 1906, National Gallery of Canada), Emanuel Hahn's *Chief Thundercloud* (1917, National Gallery of Canada), Louis-Philippe Hébert's *Pecheur à la Nigogue* which stands before the Quebec Legislature, and Suzor-Côté's *Caughnawaga Women* (1925, Art Gallery of Ontario and other collections). In the United States, the sculptor Malvina Hoffman began her commission for 104 sculptures representing "the living races of man" for the Field Museum of Natural History in Chicago in 1931.[54] Both Frances Loring and Florence Wyle worked on "record figures" for the National Museum of Man in the late 1930s, and a number of "Indian" and "Eskimo" heads (some painted rather unrealistically) survive from this period.

Loring pointed out later that "Dr. Jenness of the National Museum in Ottawa [who presumably commissioned the work] would not permit me to work from models or photographs when I did some Indian figures for him. The Indians of today have no longer pure tribal characteristics, he said."[55] It was no doubt done speculatively, with no immediate purpose other than the sculptor's satisfaction. *Eskimo Mother* was carved in stone in 1958 and bought by the National Gallery of Canada in 1960. It was one of her favourite works. Another favourite was the colossal *Goal Keeper*, which she had done several years earlier, and which was representative of the quintessential Canadian sport (Cat. No. 56). Although there was talk of casting *Goal Keeper* in the 1960s, when the National Hockey Hall of Fame was built,[56]

and of having a version carved as early as 1945, the hulking seven-foot figure, fragile in spite of its size, has never been put into permanent form.

In 1942, the International Business Machines Company wished to purchase ten pieces of Canadian sculpture for its collection, "Art of the Western Hemisphere," which was to travel extensively in the United States and South America. Many of the Canadian sculptors involved chose natives as symbols of their country. Frances Loring carved a wooden head, which she called *Eskimo Woman*.[57]

Canadian fauna was also represented in the work of the Girls. It was a natural subject for Florence Wyle, who was a fervent animal and nature lover, as her poetry indicates. In addition to her work for the Canadian approach plaza to the Rainbow Bridge, and her *Deer Panel* for Baron Byng High School, she represented in sculpted form a number of smaller creatures, such as cats (Cat. No. 79), dogs, and ducks. The elegant form of *Blue Heron* (Cat. Nos. 51a and 51b) was cast twice in stone, and once in bronze for use as fountain sculpture. During the 1930s other sculptors, including Thoreau MacDonald, Emanuel Hahn, Sydenham P. Harvey, and Jacobine Jones, also turned to animals in their search for typically Canadian subject matter.

Finally, in addition to the native groups they modelled for the National Museum in the 1930s, Loring and Wyle portrayed Canada through the many types of people who live in this country. *The Miner* (Cat. No. 60) was done in response to news of a mining disaster at Moose River that occurred in 1936 in which three men were trapped for three days. Frances Loring had always been interested in mining (her father, it should be remembered, was a mining engineer). Loring's portrait of *Sir Frederick Banting* (Cat. No. 55)

is one of her strongest portraits. She believed it to be one of the best things she had ever done and said that "Dr. Banting himself was very pleased with it and said he would not pose for anyone else."[58] It became in a way, the official portrait of Banting and was reproduced many times. Loring endeavoured to express the strength of Banting's personality by emphasizing his strong features; in the "double portrait" (Figure 53) of Frances Loring and the Banting bust, the strong physiognomy of the sculptor is a match for that of Banting. Loring described enough of the physical details of her sitter to make the head recognizable as a portrait, then selectively emphasized certain forms to interpret the spirit within. She recounted in an interview with Elspeth Chisholm of the Canadian Broadcasting Corporation how she would do "two heads, one from the sitter and one from her head." It is those elements drawn "from her head" that create the resemblance among the heads, whether portraits or otherwise. Many share a square jaw, long chin, and full lips—unmistakable Loring trade marks.

Soon after Banting was killed in a plane crash in February 1941, Loring wrote to the National Gallery to suggest that more copies be made of the Banting portrait. The director, H.O. McCurry, replied that they had no money for purchases, these funds having been cut off during wartime. In 1948, Loring broached the subject with Martin Baldwin, director of the Art Gallery of Toronto, and found him receptive to the idea of acquiring a copy of the head; he also thought he could help her make further sales[59]. She limited the total number of bronze casts to five. By April 1949, the Art Gallery of Toronto, the National Gallery of Canada, and the University of Toronto were in a position to purchase one bronze each, for two thousand dollars, which they did; five were finally cast that year by the Gorham Company, in Providence, Rhode Island, and one later in 1966.[60]

The great demand for sculpture that began after the First World War and lasted through the 1920s fell off rapidly in the Depression and during the Second World War. The careers of Frances Loring and Florence Wyle reflect, in general, the vicissitudes of the Canadian sculptor's life from 1920 to 1948. Those who lacked resourcefulness and adaptability did not survive as sculptors. In the 1950s, gravel was discovered on their Rouge River property and they sold the land. With the proceeds the Girls were able at last to make major renovations to the Studio in 1952, and to live more comfortably. Loring wrote: "This is an austere and forbidding country for a sculptor. There are no patrons to make the road easy and very few of the buying public are able to recognize real merit from charlatanism."[61] While the Girls gradually lost their place in the forefront of Canadian sculpture in the years following the Second World War, they continued to undertake major projects up until the end of the 1950s.

ENDNOTES

1. The studio was not adequately heated until further additions and renovations were made in 1952; the fireplace and a Quebec heater bought from a station agent were not enough to heat the high, vaulted room. The dining room, bathroom, and kitchen were located in the basement; Wyle's bedroom was in the former vestry; and Loring apparently had a lean-to affair in the former nave. They were known as "the cheerful children of the chilly church." The novelty of the "home-studio" attracted the press; articles ran in the *Mail and Empire* (November 20, 1920) and the *Star* (November 27, 1920). The studio was designated as a historic site in 1976 by the Ontario Historical Society. In 1984, the city of Toronto, at the request of the Moore Park Residents' Association, honoured the Girls by having four pieces of their work cast and installed in the parkette at the north-east corner of St. Clair Avenue and Mount Pleasant Road, which was newly named the Loring-Wyle parkette.

2. Goldman acknowledged the help of Frances Loring and Florence Wyle in her autobiography, *Living my Life* (New York: Dover Publications, 1970, pp. 990, 992), although she transposes their names. These lectures were a great success, as one headline indicates: "Brilliant Disquisition on Ibsen by Emma Goldman," Toronto Daily *Star*, November 30, 1926.

3. Eric Brown to M.K. Turner, Office of the City Clerk, Fort William, Ontario, February 8, 1922. National Gallery of Canada Archives File 05.1.

4. Minutes of the Annual Meeting of the OSA, March 9, 1920. OSA Minutes Book, January 1916 to March 1931, Archives of Ontario. They had been nominated in February by C.W. Jefferys.

5. Loring's first recorded lecture was in 1921, for the Three Arts Club, held at the Women's Union at the University of Toronto. She was a frequent lecturer at the WAA on subjects such as war memorials (1922), garden sculpture (1924), modern sculpture (1927), and "sculptural development" (1934). Both Loring and Wyle gave talks at the Art Gallery of Toronto, Loring in 1932 as one of six speakers addressing the theme of "The artists' contribution to life" and Wyle in 1933 on great artists in different countries. In 1939 the CBC scheduled a series of talks on great sculptors by Loring, which included "Michelangelo and the Greeks"; "Rodin and his Time"; "Bourdelle and Mestrovic"; "Epstein and some moderns"; "Sculpture in the United States"; and "Canadian sculpture."

6. Louis V. Hunter, "New Woman Academician Has Her Studio in an Abandoned Church," *Ottawa Evening Citizen*, November 24, 1938.

7. Robert Shipley, in an unpublished study on Canadian war memorials entitled "To Mark our Place," states that sixty-six per cent of the twelve hundred monuments he has recorded were built soon after the First World War. In possession of the author, Robert Shipley.

8. Shipley. Hahn apparently did some work for the Thomson Monument Company, which was responsible for erecting these monuments. Similar monuments may be found in Bolton and Cornwall in Ontario, and in Gaspé, Québec. One bronze version exists in Westville, Nova Scotia, and it alone bears Hahn's signature.

9. Letter from Frances Loring to Eric Brown, October 17, 1922. National Gallery Archives, File 5.42 Loring.

10. This was prompted by the injustice done to Elizabeth Wyn Wood who, after having fairly won the Winnipeg War Memorial Competition in 1927, was denied the commission because her husband, Emanuel Hahn, was German-born. Hahn had come first in an earlier competition for the same memorial and had been disqualified because his heritage was viewed as inappropriate.

11. In an undated letter to Eric Brown in the summer of 1919, Frances Loring wrote: "We have wasted a lot of time on fool monuments that we would have preferred putting on war records." National Gallery Archives, 5.42 - L Canadian War Artists.

12. "General Conditions for the Guidance of Architects, Artists and Sculptors in Preparing Competitive designs for the proposed National Commemorative War Monument for the Dominion of Canada in Ottawa, Canada, February 12, 1925." Public Archives of Canada, Ottawa, RG11, Vol. 4004 File 9238-1-A.

13. Loring's written description of her entry was as follows: "On the face of the shaft emerging from the stone is a male figure of Victory with the Sword of Sacrifice / underneath is the inscription- 'To the unconquered Dead' / On the opposite face is a female mourning figure also emerging from the stone with the inscription underneath: 'These died that Mankind might be Free' / At the sides are groups explaining the sacrifice made by the women—the mothers and nurses."

14. Contract between the Law Society of Upper Canada and Anna Loring [sic], September 15, 1926. Archives of the Law Society of Upper Canada, Osgoode Hall,

Toronto.

15. Letter to Eric Brown from Frances Loring, January 27, 1928. National Gallery of Canada Archives File 7.1 Loring.

16. This is not adequately documented. When Ira Lake, who was originally contracted to supply the carved decoration for the chamber, broke his contract, the firm of Balmer and Blakely of Toronto took on the work. Their tender was officially accepted at the end of August, 1927. This included supplying the plaster cast of three figures and a decorated tympanum, which they probably subcontracted to Loring shortly thereafter. See letter to John Pearson from Balmer and Blakely, August 9, 1927. Public Archives of Canada, Ottawa, RG2 Series I Vol. 2675 1575-70.

17. Public Archives of Canada, Ottawa, RG11 Vol. 2689 Files 1575-99.

18. Excerpt from an essay entitled "Sculpture and the People," written by Wyle in December, 1943, for *Canadian Art* magazine. Walter Abell, the editor, returned it to her. He had hoped that she would treat the subject in relation to modern democracy and comment on "the progress made in problems involved in bringing sculpture into closer touch with the people of the modern world." Wyle, however, had taken a historical approach. The essay (Env. 87) and the letter from Abell to Wyle, dated February 28, 1944 (Env. 88) are contained in the archival material from the Loring and Wyle estates, housed in the E.P. Taylor Reference Library, Art Gallery of Ontario.

19. In his chapter on American sculpture between the wars, Wayne Craven (*Sculpture in America*, rev. ed, Newark: University of Delaware Press, 1984, p. 554) states that the key to sculpture in America at that time was the theory of simplification and abstraction of natural form. He points out that American art followed a more moderate course than that of European art during the same period. Canadians tended to follow the course of their neighbours to the south. They were often exposed to exhibitions of the more conservative moderns, organized by American institutions and shown in Canada.

20. Two French sculptors, Emile Antoine Bourdelle (1861-1929) and Aristide Maillol (1861-1944), the Yugoslavian Ivan Mestrovic (1883-1962), and the American Paul Manship (1885-1966) were all represented at exhibitions held at the Art Gallery of Toronto in the 1920s. All were well-known in North America by 1927.

21. It was noted at the time ("The Toronto Art Gallery—New Extensions to be opened shortly bring it to Metropolitan Dimensions," *Saturday Night*, January 9, 1926) that the new sculpture court was only half its projected size; it was to be extended northwards to double its length. The architecture firm Darling and Pearson won an award for their design of the court in 1927.

22. Ivan Mestrovic was highly regarded in Toronto in the late 1920s. *Mother at Prayer* was presented to the Gallery by Mrs. Timothy Eaton in 1928. The Art Gallery was congratulated on this new acquisition in the *Canadian Forum* (Vol. 8, No. 89, February 1928, p. 525): "Mestrovic has been widely praised as 'The most significant, the most original, and the most extraordinary of living sculptors . . .' He should help us greatly in the forming of a local standard." Emanuel Hahn delivered a lecture on Mestrovic at a monthly OSA meeting in May, 1925 (attended by Loring and Wyle), and *Saturday Night* later ran a lengthy article entitled "The Art of Ivan Mestrovic" in 1927 (Vol. 42, No. 24, April 30, 1927, p. 3). Loring, a great admirer of Mestrovic, visited him at the University of Syracuse where he taught, and corresponded with him in the 1950s concerning an exhibition of his work being organized by the National Gallery of Canada.

Other works acquired in 1928 included Rodin's *Eve*, *Adam*, and the terra-cotta *Head of Pierre de Wiessant*; Manship's *Diana* and *Actaeon*; and Epstein's *R.B. Cunningham Grahame*.

23. A conservative critic, Bridle would have appreciated this. "Big Crowds, Seven Shows as Art Gallery Reopens," Toronto Daily Star, October 6, 1928.

24. See Albert E. Elsen, *The Partial Figure in Modern Sculpture: from Rodin to 1969* (Baltimore: The Baltimore Museum of Art, 1969), p. 33.

25. See Susan Rather, "The Past Made Modern: Archaism in American Sculpture," *Arts Magazine* Vol. 59, No. 3 (November 1984), pp. 111–119.

26. Bertram Brooker, "Sculpture's New Mood," in *Yearbook of the Arts in Canada 1928-9* (Toronto: MacMillan, 1929), p. 102. Ongoing reports were made throughout the 1920s of the treasures being found in the Tomb of Tutenkhamen, which was first discovered in 1922. The Egyptian Gallery at the Royal Ontario Museum was opened in 1930.

27. Eric Brown wrote to Florence Wyle to tell her of their interest in the sculpture, and to express the hope that the National Gallery would have the first opportunity of considering it again if it were cut in stone or marble "of a colour not unlike the

plaster which seems to suit it very well." February 25, 1931. Curatorial Files, National Gallery of Canada Archives, *Torso* 4087.

28. Letter from Florence Wyle to Eric Brown, April 19, 1932, Curatorial Files, National Gallery of Canada Archives, *Torso* 4087.

29. Letter from Eric Brown to J.O. Marchand, April 13, 1933, Curatorial Files, National Gallery of Canada Archives, *Torso* 4087.

30. Fred H. Brigden, "The 56 Annual Exhibition of the RCA," Royal Architectural Institute of Canada *Journal*, Vol. 13, No. 12 (December 1936), p. 222.

31. Minutes of the monthly meeting of the OSA, April 4, 1933. Minute Book, March 1931–April 1937, Archives of Ontario MU 2255.

32. Letter from Frances Loring, secretary of the SSC, to W.P. O'Meara, Department of the Secretary of State, January 23, 1932. Public Archives of Canada, Ottawa, SSC Papers MG 28 I 185, Vol. I.

33. Letter from Frances Loring to Eric Brown, June 29, 1935. National Gallery of Canada Archives, 5.5 S Exhibitions in Gallery SSC.

34. Letter from Frances Loring to the Honorable Mr. P.J.A. Cardin, Minister of Public Works, November 20, 1935. Public Archives of Canada RG11 Vol. 2711 2556-20B.

35. Elizabeth Wyn Wood, "Observations on a Decade: 1938–48 Ten Years of Canadian Sculpture," RAIC *Journal*, Vol. 25, No. 1 (January 1948), pp. 15–19, p. 30.

36. Minutes of a regular meeting of the SSC, June 3, 1946. Public Archives of Canada, SSC Papers MG 28 I 185, Vol. 1.

37. Around 1929, Florence Wyle was asked by her friend Anne Savage to undertake this panel for the library of Baron Byng High School in Montreal, where Savage taught. It was to complement the murals, which Savage herself had painted, and a relief by sculptor Philippe Hébert. The panel in the Collection of the Art Gallery of Ontario is a copy of the Baron Byng panel, no longer in situ, owned by the Protestant School Board of Greater Montreal.

38. Frances Loring, "Sculpture in the Garden," *Canadian Art*, Vol. 1, No. 2 (December–January 1943–1944), pp. 64–66.

39. Around 1935 Wyle designed a memorial tablet for the late Mrs. Timothy Eaton, which was installed in the nave of the Timothy Eaton Memorial Church.

40. See Michele H. Bogart, "American Garden Sculpture: A new perspective," in *Fauns and Fountains: American Garden Statuary, 1890–1930* (Southampton, New York: The Parrish Art Museum, 1985), unpag.

41. See Geoffrey Hunt, *John M. Lyle: Toward a Canadian Architecture* (Kingston: Agnes Etherington Art Centre, 1982).

42. Eric Arthur, "Sculpture in Building," RAIC *Journal*, Vol. 15, No. 6 (June 1938), p. 130.

43. Letter from Frances Loring to H.O. McCurry, February 28, 1941. National Gallery Archives 7.1 Loring.

44. Pearl McCarthy, "Art and Artists," *Globe and Mail*, August 13, 1942.

45. Letter from Florence Wyle to William J. Wood, June 9, 1947. Courtesy A. Walling Ruby, Toronto.

46. The appearance of the interior cannot be reconstructed because of the absence of installation photos. Photographs of sketches by Florence Wyle indicate that she may have been responsible for two of the four interior reliefs, which personified the times of day. The Girls may have been aware that Michelangelo had used a similar theme in the Medici Chapel. Like his allegorical figures, those of the Girls' embodied the destiny that rules the lives of mortals, and in a banking hall, a temple of commerce, they served as a *memento mori*.

When the Bank was demolished in 1972, the exterior reveal panels were rescued by the late Spencer Clark. They form part of his collection of architectural sculpture at the Guild Inn, Scarborough, Ontario.

47. G. Stephen Vickers, "The Architecture in Sculpture," RAIC *Journal*, Vol. 26, No. 1 (January 1949), pp. 28–31.

48. Pearl McCarthy, "Bank of Montreal Panels soon adopted by Citizens," *Globe and Mail*, September 3, 1949.

49. Lenore Crawford, "Fifty Years of Sculpture: Loring and Wyle at the London Public Library and Art Museum," *Canadian Art*, Vol. XX, No. 2 (March–April 1963), p. 79.

50. "Women with Mallets: Loring and Wyle complete three decades of partnership in sculpture," *New World Illustrated* (February 1942).

51. Letter from the director, National Gallery of Canada, to Dr. Charles Camsell, deputy minister, Department of Mines, Ottawa, November 21, 1926. National Gallery Archives File 5.5 West Coast Art.

52. "At the Grange Craft Shop," unidentified clipping, Art Gallery of Ontario scrapbook October 6, 1928–December 31, 1929, Art Gallery of Ontario Archives. The shop was an "interesting new venture" by students of the Ontario College of Art and was run on a cooperative basis.

The totem also made its appearance in

the form of architectural sculpture around 1930, notable examples being John Lyle's Runnymede Branch Library and the William H. Wright Building by Mathers and Haldenby (demolished), where decorative relief panels featuring totem-pole imagery flanked the entrance.

53. My thanks to Maia-Mari Sutnik, for identifying the photographer and the publications in which the picture was reproduced.

54. See Linda Nochlin, "Malvina Hoffman: A Life in Sculpture," *Arts Magazine*, Vol. 59, No. 3 (November 1984), pp. 106–110.

55. Lyn Harrington, "Unique Church Studio is Home and Workshop," *Saturday Night*, November 18, 1944, pp. 4–5. They were working on the figures in 1938, according to an article in the Timmins *Press* (Louis V. Hunter, "Has Studio in small unused Toronto Church," November 26, 1938).

56. See letter from Chips (Hugh) Allward to Charles S. Band, April 27, 1962, discussing the possibility of having a cast of *Goal Keeper* made. Charles Band approached the mayor of Toronto, Philip G. Givens, but received a negative response (letter from Givens to Band, April 15, 1964). Loring and Wyle Archives, E.P. Taylor Reference Library, Art Gallery of Ontario. See also Paul Duval, "A Monument to Don," the *Telegram*, November 30, 1963. In 1945 Loring had been about to sell a *Goal Keeper* in stone to Maple Leaf Gardens for $3,000. The deal must have fallen through. See letter from Frances Loring to H.O. McCurry, March 5, 1945. National Gallery Archives, Correspondence 7.1-L, Loring.

57. It was number forty in the catalogue *Sculpture of the Western Hemisphere*, published by International Business Machines in 1942. The piece was bought by the Plaza Galleries in New York in 1960; its present whereabouts is unknown.

58. Letter from Frances Loring to H.O. McCurry, February 28, 1941. National Gallery Archives 7.1 Loring. She also designed his tombstone, which is in the Mount Pleasant Cemetery, Toronto.

59. Letter from Frances Loring to Martin Baldwin, May 7, 1948. Art Gallery of Ontario, Accession File *Head of Frederick Banting*.

60. One of the original five found its way to McMaster University; another was sold to an art dealer, and is now privately owned. When the University of British Columbia approached Loring in the 1960s to enquire about obtaining a copy, a sixth cast was made.

61. Letter from Frances Loring to Mr. Csaplar, December 9, 1962. Courtesy of Mrs. Richard Hungerford.

FIGURE 56.
Frances Loring, Florence Wyle, and Sylvia
Daoust. *The Calvert Drama Trophies*, 1953. Photo
by Pringle and Booth, Limited. Photo: gift of
the Estates of Frances Loring and Florence Wyle,
1983.

four

LATER WORK AND FURTHER CONTRIBUTIONS 1948–1968

Around 1950, Frances Loring was still considered one of Canada's best sculptors—"a traditional sculptor of great power."[1] The names Loring and Wyle continued to appear with some regularity in the press, for they were still receiving noteworthy commissions. Frances Loring carried on as an active spokesperson for and supporter of sculpture in Canada. During the fifties, they received some recognition for their artistic contributions: Florence Wyle was a recipient of the Coronation Medal in 1953, and Frances Loring was awarded a gold medal by the University of Alberta for "long and conspicuous service to the arts" in 1954 and an honorary Doctor of Laws from the University of Toronto the following year.

They were soon to be eclipsed, however, by a new generation of sculptors working in a tradition rooted in Surrealist sculpture of the 1930s, whose use of the "found object" took sculpture into the realms of conceptual art. Having been trained in the late nineteenth century when sculpture was defined as the fine art of modelling, carving, and casting and its prime subject was the human figure, the Girls clung to a romantic definition of sculpture. Wyle wrote: "A sculptor is one who sees and understands the beauty and

dignity of natural form—in man and in all life even in the growth of a plant and whose interest has led him to study and acquire the technique necessary to portray these harmonious forms in clay and wood and in the more enduring mediums of stone and bronze" (completed form for Vocational Guidance Centre, 1957). Loring stated that "Sculpture is the artist's analysis of life in terms of three dimensions and in terms of silence. It is the symbol of the artist's visual experience concentrated in visual form" ("Frances Loring, sculptor, gives interesting talk on art," Ottawa Evening *Journal*, February 8, 1950). But these definitions excluded Loring and Wyle from active participation in the forefront of new sculptural developments, for they could not be reconciled with the redefinition of sculpture, which involved new ways of working with new materials, and new concepts of forms in space.

The 1950s represented a period of hiatus in sculpture. In 1950, contemporary Canadian sculpture was described as "cautious and conservative," and the approach taken by most sculptors criticized for being "too unassumingly naturalist to be regarded as 'contemporary.' "[2] Frances Loring recognized the 1950s as a slack period in her own career,

and welcomed the opportunity to embark on a lecture tour of northern Alberta with A.Y. Jackson in the fall of 1952, commenting, "I do very much need to get away and brush off some cobwebs."[3] This is not to say that either she or Florence Wyle was inactive at that time; on the contrary, Loring was on the developmental committee of the SSC as of 1949, and helped Elizabeth Wyn Wood to prepare the SSC's brief to the Massey Commission (the Royal Commission on the Development of the Arts, Letters and Sciences 1949–1951), while sitting on the Art Gallery of Toronto's Canadian Collection Committee (1950–1955)[4] and helping the National Gallery to organize an exhibition of the work of Ivan Mestrovic in 1951. Florence Wyle undertook two reliefs for the Alberta Red Cross Crippled Children's Hospital in Calgary, (Cat. Nos. 81 and 82) designed by their old colleague W.L. Somerville in 1950, and a large relief of farm animals for the McNabb Memorial Library at the Ontario Agricultural College in Guelph, in 1954. Loring put most of her energies into public life, which also included frequent lectures; Florence Wyle withdrew into her work, and, beginning in the late 1940s, began carving small torsos in sumac, starting with a series known as *Rivers*

FIGURE 54.

The ten *Rivers of America* on display at the
studio, c. 1950. Photo: gift of the Estates of
Frances Loring and Florence Wyle, 1983.

of America (Cat. No. 77; Figures 54 and 55).

Wyle had carved torsos in wood earlier
(Cat. Nos. 59 and 73), but the Rivers series
is quite different. She went beyond earlier
works and exploited the wood to its fullest by
using the strong grain of the sumac to define
individual forms, the concentric rings around
the breasts and belly in *The Platte* and *The
Hudson*, for example, and by allowing an element of "non finito" to enter the work. For
example, with some of the outer bark un-
touched, as in *The Illinois*, the figure appears
to emerge from its woody sheath, a sort of
Daphne in reverse. Of all the rivers, *The
Hudson* (Figure 55) most strongly maintains
the cylindrical shape of the tree. Although
Wyle may not have been aware of it, a prec-
edent for her small wooden figures had been
set by the early American sculptor William
Rush, who carved his life-size *Allegory of the
Schuylkill River* (also known as *Water Nymph
and Bittern*) around 1809 in pine.[5]

With the Rivers and with other carved
figures of the period, both Loring and Wyle
returned to themes and motifs they had used
earlier as solutions to formal problems. For
example, in *Illinois* and in two figures, *Spring*
(Cat. No. 83, Pl. No. 8) and *Summer*
(Cat. No. 85), Wyle encircled the lower
extremities of the figure with a piece of drapery
connected to one of the hands, as in *Study
of a Girl* (1926; (Cat. Nos. 32 and 50), in this
case by slicing through the trunk at an
oblique angle. The modest pose used in *Spring*
had been used earlier in one of two pieces
known as *Young Girl* (c. 1938), a posthumous
cast of which resides in the Loring-Wyle
parkette.

There were ten rivers altogether in the
series, which Wyle had hoped to sell as a unit,
but which were ultimately sold separately
and dispersed in private collections across the
country. Before they were sold, however,
and while the series was on display at a Toronto gallery, they were viewed by two of the
executive members of the Dominion Drama
Festival, who were looking for suitable trophies
for their annual regional winners and for a
final award for the best among the regional
winners. Pauline McGibbon (Cat. No. 95),
who was to be lieutenant-governor of Ontario
from 1974 to 1980, and David Ongley, QC,
president of the festival,[6] had been advised by
painter A.J. Casson to see the small carvings,
after an attempt to procure a design for the
festival trophy had failed. In 1953, Loring,
Wyle, and Sylvia Daoust of Montreal were
commissioned to carve fourteen trophies,
which symbolized the various influences on the
theatre (Figure 56). They were financed by
the sponsor of the festival, Calvert Distilleries,
who gave their name to the first prize in the
festival, the Calvert Trophy (renamed the
Dominion Drama Festival Final Festival Trophy in 1960, when Calvert withdrew their
sponsorship). The trophy had been carved by
Florence Wyle, and was known as *Drama*
(Cat. No. 87). A fifteenth trophy was carved
by Wyle in 1958, when a new region was
added to the festival's roster.

Two trophies, *Truth* and *Poetry*, followed
closely on the model of Wyle's rivers. *Poetry*
appears to "emerge from the block." Both are
in sumac, and are more stylized than the
other trophies she carved. *Drama* and *Wisdom*
(Cat. No. 86) recall the classical repose of
the Greek *kouroi*, which Wyle had effectively
captured earlier in *American Family* (c. 1938;
Cat. No. 63). Elements of earlier work also
mark one of Frances Loring's pieces, *Invocation* (Cat. No. 89), which is a close reworking
of a plaster of the same title (c. 1930;
Cat. No. 49). Her *Faun* (Cat. No. 88) is the
most imaginative of a generally static group

of carvings.

Frances Loring's last major commission of importance was for the monument, on Parliament Hill, to Robert L. Borden, prime minister of Canada from 1911 to 1920. When the competition was announced in April, 1953, she submitted a design consisting of a pedestal and two steps to be erected in granite, with a figure of Sir Robert Borden to be in bronze. She provided two options for the figure, one holding the seals of Canada's full autonomy in one hand (Cat. No. 91), the other showing him in a characteristic pose with both hands behind his back (Cat. No. 92). She was guided by photographs of Borden, the proposed site, and the statue of Laurier across from which Borden was to be placed, which were provided at her request by the government. Her small model (Cat. No. 91) was selected, with one by Jean Meroz (1911–   ), from among twenty-four competitors (one was Florence Wyle) in the late fall of 1953, and she was asked to submit a larger model (Cat. No. 93) by the end of March, 1954. On the basis of the larger model, "with a few modifications," she was awarded the commission in December, 1954. Of the figure, she commented: "I have modelled the fighting Borden not only of the war years but of the postwar period when, under his leadership, Canada took her position as a nation in the peace conference. Therefore, he stands firmly on both feet."[7]

The next step was to make a half-size model (Figure 57). At this stage, Loring went into more detailed research on the accuracy of the likeness and on clothing and accessories. Two of the three judges also had suggestions. (The judges were John Bland, head of the Department of Architecture at McGill University; W.G. Constable, former assistant director of the National Gallery of London;

and Sylvia Daoust (1902–1974), who was ill at the time the final decision was made.) Bland and Constable suggested that the head and shoulders be made more like those of Borden (Borden's private secretary, who had known him for years, felt that Loring's model was not "rugged" enough); that the shoulders be squared; that the boots and trousers be given more character and refinement; that the back view be made more interesting; and that the lettering of the inscription on the base be in Roman capitals, such as those used on the arches of Titus and Constantine, which were characterized by an "incised V." Finally, they thought that the figure, wearing an overcoat and standing in the open air, was an inappropriate one to be holding the great seal. A large pair of fur gloves on such a figure would be more appropriate![8]

Frances argued that the likeness and figure characteristics would be worked out in the larger model. She was adamant that the inclusion of a scroll or seal was not out of keeping with the overcoat or the pose; nor did she want to change the simpler style of lettering, which she felt was appropriate for carving in granite.[9] The finished monument shows that she made some compromises, but she followed her own wishes on the whole. The aggressive-looking figure is certainly powerful, and more attention has been given to the costume. But he is holding a sheaf of papers—signifying his role at the Versailles Peace Conference—not gloves, and the lettering is a simple Roman capital, as Loring had suggested. It was unveiled on January 8, 1957, later than originally planned; it cost fifty thousand dollars (Figure 58).[10]

With one exception, no other monument commissions came her way. A number of portraits were done in the later years by both

FIGURE 55.
Florence Wyle. *The Hudson River*, c. 1949. Sumac, dimensions unknown. Private collection. Photo by Jean Gainfort Merrill. Photo: gift of the Estates of Frances Loring and Florence Wyle, 1983.

Loring and Wyle: notably Ira Dilworth, Barbara Anne Robertson (founder of Mothercraft), and Eleanor Sniderman by Wyle; and John W. Billes, E.B. Barber, and the hands of Dr. Herbert Bruce by Loring. Executed in the early 1960s, when Loring was suffering from arthritis, these are not among her strongest works. The one exception to portraiture was Frances Loring's full-scale relief of a mother and her children for the Women's Building at the Canadian National Exhibition in 1957 (Figure 59), again an architecturally-related work. It was done with great physical effort, for not only was arthritis a problem, but by that time, Loring had also gained a considerable amount of weight, which made climbing up and down scaffolding increasingly difficult. The group marks a return to an earlier theme (see *War Widow and Children*, c. 1928; Cat. No. 34) of a mother in a timeless costume of flowing robes sheltering two small children. As she had done before, Loring probably asked Wyle to sculpt the figures of the children.

The most significant feature about the relief is the material in which it was cast, a weather-resistant polyester, which was less than half the cost of bronze. While commenting that this was a large work in a material not used before, Loring credited others (Dora de Pedery-Hunt[11] (b. 1913), and Jack de Maria) with having made experiments in the medium, which had given her the courage to try it.[12] De Pedery-Hunt was also one of the artists of foreign birth, or "New Canadians," whom Alan Jarvis credited in a 1962 editorial in *Canadian Art* with having brought to Canada old traditions of craftsmanship along with new images and forms, and with contributing to the establishment of international standards here.[13] In the same issue of *Canadian Art*, which was specially devoted to Canadian

sculpture, Jarvis also wrote that only in the 1950s were Canadian sculptors finding a new lease on life. The reawakening, which began at the end of the 1950s, did not become visible until the early 1960s. He noted the blurring of traditional boundary lines between painting and sculpture, observing that the conventional categories of carvers and modellers had little to do with current work, a good percentage of which involved welding. As might be expected, the Girls felt that welding belonged in the factory, and had little sympathy for the most recent developments in sculpture.

Regardless of Wyle's view that creativity in sculpture had very narrow limits, and that innovations could be made only in terms of subject matter,[15] it is evident from their tendency to fall back on earlier solutions to aesthetic problems, reworking old themes in a new context, that there had been few new ideas in their work for a number of years. Around 1958, they began a stock-taking of their careers by suddenly recording previously undocumented works, many of which were still in their possession at the Studio. They expressed the desire to have a few things put in permanent material "so that they may outlive us."[16] In 1957 Florence Wyle had an earlier piece carved in marble for the Art Gallery of Toronto at the request of the director, Martin Baldwin; *Draped Torso* (Cat. No. 70) had remained in plaster form ever since it had first been exhibited at the New York World's Fair in 1939. Wyle felt it to be "one of her best."[17] In a film made by Christopher Chapman in 1965 for the CBC programme "Telescope," Wyle is shown refining the surface of *Sea and Shore* (Cat. No. 80), a piece that had been inspired by a waterfall around 1950, but which was not carved in marble until 1965.[18] In 1959,

Ryerson Press published a small book of the poems she had written and collected over the years, and about 1964, the Girls discussed their desire to have a book published that would record their careers and creative achievements.[19]

It was not until 1966, the year the Girls were hospitalized, that the heads of Fred Varley (an earlier cast had been bought by the National Gallery in 1956) and Vincent Massey (modelled in 1930) were cast in bronze by the Pollock Gallery to fill orders placed at the highly successful exhibition of the Girls' work held there in January 1966.[20] Wyle attended the opening; Loring was hospitalized; neither was well enough to appreciate the show's success. In 1965 Loring had written to Roman Bronze Works, which had handled much of their bronze casting in the past, to request estimates for works she most wanted to see in permanent form. These included a piece called *The Hound of Heaven* (cast in 1967), *Grief* (Cat. No. 15), *Girl with Fish* (Cat. No. 53), *Turkey*, and the famous *Goal Keeper* (Cat. No. 56). A number of pieces, including *Turkey*, *Miner* (Cat. No. 60), and *The Old One* (Cat. No. 8), were cast in 1968, after Loring's death; the high cost of casting *Goal Keeper*, however, was prohibitive. In 1969, eleven more works were cast, after a second major show of their work at the Pollock Gallery.[21] Among them were *Mother of the Race*, *Portrait of Varley*, and *Study of a Young Girl*.

The commissions stopped coming in, and their healths began to decline, when Frances Loring and Florence Wyle drew up wills in 1963. The contents of these wills, which mirror each other in every aspect except where family was concerned, underline their life-long commitment to Canadian sculpture, which had guided so many of their activities.

This is summarized in the first clause, which states that the wills were made ". . . upon the mutual wish and desire to assist and encourage Canadian Sculpture and by means of gifts to public Art Galleries, public Museums and institutions of learning across Canada, to afford to the people of Canada particularly, the opportunity of seeing, appreciating and enjoying the work of Canadian sculptors."[22]

A group calling themselves the Friends of Loring and Wyle recognized the Girls' desire to promote the cause of sculpture, and raised a substantial sum of money in 1963.[23] With this fund, they purchased work from the Girls to donate to the smaller regional galleries in whose collections they were not represented. It was an indirect way of offering the Girls financial support, while fulfilling one of their wishes.

In their wills, Loring and Wyle bequeathed the studio to the Royal Canadian Academy, in the hope that the academy would continue their personal practice of welcoming people—especially neighbourhood children—to the studio (Figure 60). If the academy could not use the studio as a gallery, it was to be sold; the proceeds were to be placed in a sculpture fund. The fund could also get money from the sale of any of their work not sold before their deaths. The trustees were to be advised in the sale and dispersement of these works by a "Sculptor Advisory Committee," composed of a sculptor member from both the OSA and RCA, the president of the SSC, and "from time to time" the directors of the National Gallery of Canada and the Art Gallery of Toronto.[24] The sculpture fund was to be used "to purchase works of sculpture, and whether in completed form or by commission, produced by Canadian sculptors ordinarily resident in Canada."[25] This echoes the Emily Carr Trust Fund, the trustees of which were Lawren Harris and Ira Dilworth; her deed of gift had stipulated that at least one award per year be given to a promising artist of British Columbia.

It took years to finally carry out the terms of the wills. The Royal Canadian Academy decided, largely because of zoning restrictions, that it could not keep the studio, and it was sold in 1971. Fortunately, the purchaser, who had been a friend and supporter of the Girls, was sensitive to its significance, and intended to maintain the character of the building, agreeing to store the works of art for as long as was required. The bulk of the sculpture remained in the studio until it was moved to the Art Gallery of Ontario in the fall of 1982. The proceeds from the sale of the studio went towards setting up a Royal Canadian Academy Trust Fund (the Loring and Wyle bequest was combined with those of Walter Allward and his son Hugh Allward), the purpose of which is "to enable the Academy to carry out the increasing demands upon its services to the citizens of Canada." It would be used for "special grants, scholarships, fellowships, and purchase awards to public galleries and universities, as well as for other projects designed to benefit and encourage promising young artists and to enrich the national identity of Canada and the lives of all its citizens."[26] It is not, then, strictly for the use of sculptors, but after some discussion, it was decided that the Girls had no desire to tie the academy down, and that the trustees of the fund would comply with the spirit of their bequest.[27]

The Girls died within three weeks of each other, Florence Wyle on January 13, 1968, and Frances Loring on February 3, 1968. They had both been admitted to Greenacres Home for the Aged in Newmarket in 1967, but sadly, as senility advanced, neither was able to recognize the other. Both willed their bodies to the University of Toronto, so no funeral services were held; gatherings of friends were held at the church, in their memory. The trustees then undertook to carry out their wish that the works remaining in their studio be sold, but this proved to be a difficult task. One of the executors, sculptor Frances Gage, made numerous attempts to sell the work at exhibitions held at various galleries, including the MacDonald Gallery (now the John B. Aird Gallery) at Queen's Park in 1977 and the University of Guelph in 1978. The work did not sell, as it was considered to be outdated, and consequently no income was forthcoming with which to set up the sculpture fund.

In 1980 the executors approached the Ministry of Culture and Recreation of the Ontario Government to seek advice as to what to do with the works remaining in the Estates. The Ministry turned to a number of institutions, including the Art Gallery of Ontario, for suggestions; it later offered the Gallery a small, representative group from the Estates' holdings. On the advice of the Curator of Canadian Historical Art, the Art Gallery suggested that it take all the work and assume the curatorial responsibility for its care and presentation to the public, thereby recognizing the importance of the work. In 1983 the works were gifted to the Art Gallery of Ontario, the major custodians of the province's artistic heritage, fully in the spirit of the Girls' intention that their sculpture touch the lives of many. This collection will function as a centre for the study of their work in Canada, and forms the focus for the continuing collection of historical Canadian sculpture. This exhibition and catalogue stand as records of the gift of the Estates of Frances Loring and Florence Wyle and of the major contribution they have made to the art of sculpture in Canada.

Their legacy lives on not only in their own work but also in the work of the artists they encouraged during their lifetimes, like Dora de Pedery-Hunt and Frances Gage,[28] for they set an example that sculpture was a valid pursuit in this country in spite of the inherent difficulties, particularly for a woman. More important is the fact that, while their own type of work may have lacked relevance for a younger generation of sculptors, their continuing efforts had kept the door ajar for the time when these artists were ready to cross the threshold to further advance the art of sculpture in Canada.

FIGURE 60.
Frances Loring and young friends, 1962. Photo by Dennis Colwell. The Lawrence Hayward Collection Documentary Art & Photography Division, Public Archives of Canada, Ottawa. Courtesy of Studios O. Allard Photographes Inc., Montreal.

ENDNOTES

1. Wm. S.A. Dale, "Sculpture," in *The Arts in Canada: A Stocktaking at Mid-Century* (Toronto: MacMillan, 1958), pp. 36, 41. See also Andrew Bell, "An Exhibition of Canadian Sculpture," *Canadian Art*, Vol. 5, No. 4 (Summer 1949), pp. 155–156.

2. "Contemporary Canadian Sculpture shows more caution than experiment," *Canadian Art*, Vol. 7, No. 3 (Spring 1950), p. 116.

3. Letter from Frances Loring to H.O. Mc-Curry, October 8, 1952. National Gallery Archives 7.4 Jackson/Loring. A.Y. Jackson and Frances Loring left for north-west Alberta on October 20, 1952 and made stops at Dawson Creek, Beaverlodge, Peace River, Spirit River, and several other towns before ending up in Winnipeg on November 5. Here Jackson was a guest of L.L. FitzGerald, and Loring stayed with her old friend Florence Brigden and her husband. The tour was sponsored by the National Gallery of Canada and the Alberta Fine Arts Department and the Department of Provincial Economic Affairs. Loring was impressed by the freshness and enthusiasm with which the people of more isolated communities approached the subject of art. She had expressed a similar opinion in 1928 after returning from Italy: because Canadians lacked the long artistic heritage of Italy, they were not bound to slavishly following in the footsteps of earlier masters.

4. Loring was responsible for initiating the Gallery's acquisition of Elizabeth Wyn Wood's *Reef and Rainbow* (Figure 51), which she proposed at a meeting of January 23, 1950. (Minutes of the Canadian Collection Committee, Art Gallery of Ontario Archives.)

5. A posthumous bronze cast is in the Philadelphia Museum of Art, Philadelphia.

6. Both subsequently became friends of the Girls; David Ongley took on their legal affairs, and was named an executor of their estates, along with Charles Band, Frances Gage, and the Canada Permanent Trust Company.

7. Pearl McCarthy, "Contest-winning sculptor to model fighting Borden," *The Globe and Mail*, December 29, 1954.

8. Letter containing comments of the judges, from H.O. McCurry to Frances Loring, December 10, 1954. National Gallery of Canada Archives 7.5 Borden.

9. Letter from Frances Loring to H.O. Mc-Curry, December 22, 1954. National Gallery of Canada Archives 7.5 Borden.

10. The government also paid the premium on an insurance policy, on Frances Loring's life, for $10,000, perhaps because she was sixty-seven years of age in 1954.

11. Dora de Pedery-Hunt had given a demonstration of working in polyester at an SSC meeting in December, 1956.

12. Pearl McCarthy, "New Plastic Material in a Loring Sculpture," *The Globe and Mail*, June 29, 1957.

13. Alan Jarvis, "Sculpture in Canada," *Canadian Art*, No. 80 (July–August 1962), p. 269.

14. Kay Kritzwiser, "Hands that mold Beauty," the *Globe Magazine*, April 7, 1962, pp. 9–11, 14, 16–17. They were wary of Henry Moore and his followers who had made a convention of punching holes in sculpture, although they recognized his great influence.

15. In a questionnaire for the Vocational Guidance Centre completed by Wyle in 1957, she wrote under the section concerning the nature of her work: "The practical work varies little within its limits, but the subject matter which is the essence of any art work, changes with each new piece of work." In her opinion, the subject was more important than the design or the technique.

16. Letter from Florence Wyle to Norah de Pencier, January 14, 1959. Norah de Pencier Papers, Public Archives of Canada, M630 D322. My thanks to Anne Goddard for allowing me access to these recently acquired papers. De Pencier, an old friend, had sent the Girls some money for their annual Christmas party, but since they no longer entertained much, they decided to put it towards casting some of their work. Inventory lists they made around that time are contained in the Loring-Wyle Archives, E.P. Taylor Reference Library, Art Gallery of Ontario, Toronto.

17. Letter from Florence Wyle to Martin Baldwin, January 25, 1957. Art Gallery of Ontario accession file *Draped Torso*.

18. It was carved by Louis Temporale, Port Credit, Ontario who had known Loring and Wyle "long before the war." He was also responsible for roughing out Loring's *Eskimo Mother and Child* and worked on the Bank of Montreal reliefs.

19. They discussed the concept with Clare Bice, curator of the London Public Library and Art Museum. See letters from Clare Bice to Charles Band and Sophia Hungerford, February 27, 1964. Loring and Wyle Archives, E.P. Taylor Reference Library, Art Gallery of Ontario. They envisaged a book containing twenty or so pages of biographical and critical text and about forty pages of pictures. In 1960 Wyle wrote to her friend Ira Dilworth, an executive with the CBC in Vancouver, to enquire if

he had any photographs of her work. Presumably she was collecting them for the catalogue of her work that she speaks of. Ira Dilworth to Florence Wyle, Loring and Wyle Archives, E.P. Taylor Reference Library, Art Gallery of Ontario.

20. Frances Gage and David Ongley approached gallery owner Jack Pollock to act as the Girls' dealer.

21. See K. Kritzwiser, "The Girls' show to foster young talent," *The Globe and Mail*, June 2, 1969.

22. Letters probate of the last will and testament and one codicil of Florence Wyle (July 11, 1974). The wills were signed on June 20, 1963.

23. The "friends" included Sophia Hungerford, who organized the fund, Mrs. Walter Gordon, and Keith McIver, and the idea was seconded by A.Y. Jackson, Mary Jackman, and Nora de Pencier. Letter from Sophia Hungerford to Charles Band, July 11, 1963. Courtesy Mr. David Ongley. See also the *Globe and Mail*, September 28, 1963. Several regional galleries benefited from these gifts, among them the galleries in Windsor, London, Kitchener, Guelph, and Sarnia.

24. Codicil to the last will and testament of Florence Wyle 1 (a).

25. Letters probate, H (c) (ii).

26. Minutes of the Annual General Assembly of the RCA, January 26, 1974. Minutes June 28 1973–January 26, 1974, The Royal Canadian Academy of Arts, RCA, Toronto.

27. Council Meeting of the RCA, June 15, 1974. Minutes Book March 23, 1974–May 24, 1975, RCA, Toronto.

28. In a 1955 interview, de Pedery-Hunt told of her arrival in Canada from Hungary in 1948 and commented, ". . . I give thanks to your Canadian sculptor Frances Loring. She is a very kind woman, a great woman . . . she helped me get started" (Margaret Aitken, "Between you and me," Toronto *Telegram*, October 28, 1955). Frances Gage, who first met them in 1951, wrote, "I wish for every aspiring artist, the help and encouragement that these two wonderful people gave me. I was not the only artist that they helped, I was simply the last one. A sculptor, I had to be, and I was astounded to find that, through them, this profession could be accepted as worthy. Now that my physical association with "the Girls" is done, I have no regrets." Frances Gage, "My memories—Frances Loring and Florence Wyle." Personal reminiscences written at this writer's request, July 18, 1983, Art Gallery of Ontario.

FIGURE 4.
Florence Wyle. *Angel of the Pool*, 1910. Plaster,
location unknown, Photographer unknown.
Photo: gift of the Estates of Frances Loring and
Florence Wyle, 1983.

CATALOGUE
OF THE EXHIBITION

KEY TO ABBREVIATIONS

AAM
Art Association of Montreal Annual Spring Exhibition

AMT, AGT, AGO
Art Museum of Toronto (1911–1919), Art Gallery of Toronto (1920–1966), Art Gallery of Ontario (1966–present)

CNE
Fine Arts Department, Canadian National Exhibition, Toronto

LPLAM
London Public Library and Art Museum

LRAG
London Regional Art Gallery

NGC
National Gallery of Canada, Ottawa

OSA
Ontario Society of Artists Annual Exhibition (held at the Art Gallery of Toronto until and including 1967)

RCA
Royal Canadian Academy of Arts Annual Exhibition

SSC
Sculptors' Society of Canada Exhibition

VAG
Vancouver Art Gallery

WAA
The Women's Art Association of Canada, Toronto

1920 War Memorials
Exhibition of "Canadian War Memorials: New Series, Last Phase" NGC

1926 War Memorials
"An exhibition of the Canadian War Memorials" AGT

1926 Hart House
An exhibition of the work of Frances Loring and Florence Wyle, Hart House, University of Toronto

1939 New York
New York World's Fair, "Canadian Art: The CSPWC and the SSC"

1942 Eaton's
1942 SSC The Fine Art Galleries, Eaton's College Street, Toronto

1942 Print Room
"In the Print Room: Jacobine Jones, Frances Loring, Dora Wechsler, Florence Wyle" AGT

1950 Contemporary Canadian Arts
"Contemporary Canadian Arts" Joint exhibition of the RCA, CGP, OSA, CSPWC, SSC, CSGA, RAIC, The Canadian Handicrafts Guild, Canadian Guild of Potters, and Spinners and Weavers of Ontario

1962 LPLAM
"Fifty Years of Sculpture: Frances Loring and Florence Wyle. Contemporary Canadian Sculpture," London Public Library and Art Museum, London, Ontario

1976 Sisler
"The Shadow of the Year," Sisler Gallery, Toronto

1977 Queen's Park
"Loring and Wyle: A Retrospective," Mac-Donald Gallery, Queen's Park, Toronto

1978 Guelph
"Sculptures by Florence Wyle and Frances Loring," University of Guelph, Guelph, Ontario

1983 LRAG
"Visions and Victories: Ten Canadian Women Artists 1914–1945" LRAG

NOTE CONCERNING DATES: if the work is undated, an approximate date has been assigned on the basis of the first exhibition appearance (usually a plaster model). The intended final medium for the piece may have been indicated in that catalogue, but the work may never have been put into more durable form.

The exhibition histories are complete for the major exhibiting societies, but may not be as complete for smaller galleries where detailed records have not been kept or have been destroyed. If no exhibition number is indicated, none was given in the catalogue.

1.
Florence Wyle
Marble Fountain (Boy and Grapes)
1907–1908
Marble
71.0 × 94.0 × 29.0 cm
Donald F. Scalzo, Winnetka, Illinois

EXHIBITIONS: 1908 "Works by Chicago Artists," Art Institute of Chicago #328 *A Fountain* (marble)

LITERATURE: *Bulletin of the Art Institute of Chicago*, July 1908; Ill. *Arts and Decoration* I (Feb. 1911); *Women's Saturday Night*, June 20, 1914.

2.
Florence Wyle
Dancing Boy   1910
Bronze
Foundry Mark: "Roman Bronze Works (Ltd., N.Y.)"
H. 45.7 cm
National Gallery of Canada, Ottawa

EXHIBITIONS: 1910–1911 "Winter Exhibition held by the National Academy of Design at the Art Students League, New York" #97; 1912 OSA #198 *Dancing Faun*; 1912 "16th Annual Exhibition of the Society of Western Artists," Art Institute of Chicago #170; 1915 Sculpture Exhibition AMT; 1915 RCA AAM #249; 1921 "Small Paintings and Sculpture by members of the OSA" #165; 1925 "British Empire Exhibition Canadian Section of Fine Arts," Wembley, England; 1927 "Exposition d'art canadien," Musée du Jeu de Paume, Paris #253 *Jeune Danseur*

LITERATURE: *The Craftsman*, vol. 19, No. 5 (Feb. 1911), p. 452; Ill. *The International Studio* vol. 47, No. 186 (August 1912), p. xviii.

3.
Frances Loring
Lamia   c. 1911
Bronze
H. 30.7 cm
London Regional Art Gallery, Purchased from the artist by Dr. Richard Crouch, 1944

EXHIBITIONS: 1912 OSA #114; 1915 Sculpture Exhibition AMT; 1915 RCA AAM #241; 1921 OSA "Small paintings and sculpture by members of the OSA" AGT #163; 1928 SSC AGT #116; 1929 "Little Pictures by members of the OSA" #177; 1929 SSC NGC #67; 1932 J. Merritt Malloney Galleries, Toronto; 1936–7 SSC Travelling #16; 1942 Print Room; 1943 SSC London Public Library and Art Museum; 1944 SSC London #13

LITERATURE: "Girl depicts dreams in marble and bronze," *Denver Colorado News*, August 22, 1911.

4.
Florence Wyle
Frances Loring   1911
Painted plaster
Signed: "Wyle 1911"
H. 55.5 cm
Art Gallery of Ontario, Toronto, Gift of the Estates of Frances Loring and Florence Wyle, 1983

EXHIBITIONS: 1915 Sculpture Exhibition AMT; 1966 Pollock Gallery; 1969 Pollock Gallery; 1977 Queen's Park; 1978 Guelph #9

LITERATURE: *Toronto Saturday Night*, November 27, 1915 p. 3; *Canadian Collector*, vol. I (April 1966), p. 23.

5.
Frances Loring
Florence Wyle   1911
Painted plaster
Signed: "F.N. Loring 1911"
H. 53.0 cm
Art Gallery of Ontario, Toronto, Gift of the
Estates of Frances Loring and Florence Wyle,
1983

EXHIBITIONS: 1915 Sculpture Exhibition AMT;
1944 OSA AGT #105; 1966 Pollock Gallery;
1969 Pollock Gallery; 1977 Queen's Park;
1978 Guelph #5

LITERATURE: Ill. *Canadian Collector*, vol. 1
(April 1966), p. 23.

Both numbers 4 & 5 were posthumously cast
for the Loring-Wyle parkette, 1984.

6.
Florence Wyle
Candlesticks   c. 1912
Painted plaster
H. 28.0 and 26.7 cm
Mr. and Mrs. Edward J. Stuebing

EXHIBITIONS: 1915 Sculpture Exhibition AMT
Candlesticks

7.
Florence Wyle
Letter Opener   c. 1915
Bronze
Signed: "Wyle"
Foundry Mark: "Griffoul/Newark, N.J."
L. 23.4 cm
Lawrence Hayward

EXHIBITIONS: 1915 Sculpture Exhibition AMT

8.
Frances Loring
The Old One   c. 1914
Painted plaster
H. 62.5 cm
Art Gallery of Ontario, Toronto, Gift of the
Estates of Frances Loring and Florence Wyle,
1983

EXHIBITIONS: 1915 Sculpture Exhibition AMT;
1928 SSC AGT #102; 1929 SSC NGC #53;
1966 Pollock Gallery *Newsboy*; 1969 Pollock
Gallery *Newsman*; 1977 Queen's Park; 1978
Guelph #4

LITERATURE: *Toronto Saturday Night*,
November 27, 1915, p. 3.

Also known as *The Old Jew*.

9.
Florence Wyle
Newsboy   c. 1914
Painted plaster
H. 47.0 cm
Art Gallery of Ontario, Toronto, Gift of the
Estates of Frances Loring and Florence Wyle,
1983

EXHIBITIONS: 1915 Sculpture Exhibition AMT;
1969 Pollock Gallery *Man with Draped Head*;
1976 Sisler Gallery; 1977 Queen's Park; 1978
Guelph *Man with Draped Head #2*

The titles for numbers 8 and 9 were
interchangeable. Their assigned titles are
those by which they were originally known.

10.
Frances Loring
Peacock Clock   c. 1915
Bronze
Foundry Mark: "Griffoul/Newark N.J."
Signed: "Loring"
35.8 × 54.6 cm
Art Gallery of Ontario, Toronto, Gift of the
Estates of Frances Loring and Florence Wyle,
1983

11.
Florence Wyle
Baby 1915
Painted plaster
Signed: "Wyle 1915"
H. 46.5 cm
John Brunke, Toronto

12.
Frances Loring
CNE Medal 1915
struck bronze
5.4 cm × 4.2 cm
Canadian National Exhibition Archives

LITERATURE: R.W. McLachlan, "Artistic and Historic Medals Struck in Canada in the Year 1915," *American Journal of Numismatics*, Vol. 49 (1915).

13.
Florence Wyle
CNE Medal 1916
Struck gilt
5.5 cm. × 4.5 cm
Canadian National Exhibition Archives

14.
Florence Wyle
Sunworshipper   c. 1916
Bronze
Foundry Mark: "Gorham Co. Founders"
Signed: "F. Wyle Sc."
H. 68.6 cm
National Gallery of Canada, Ottawa

EXHIBITIONS: 1918 RCA AMT #201; 1924
"British Empire Exhibition, Canadian Section
of Fine Arts," Wembley, England #269;
"1927 Exposition d'art canadien" Musée du
Jeu de Paume, Paris #257; 1929 SSC NGC
#115; 1983 LRAG #55

LITERATURE: Ill. H.C., "Contemporary
Canadian Sculpture–Extensive and Varied
Display at Toronto Art Gallery," *Saturday
Night*, October 27, 1928; Ill. B. Brooker,
ed. *Yearbook of the Arts in Canada 1928–9*,
Plate VI; Ill. Natalie Luckyj, "Visions and
Victories, Canadian Women Artists 1914–
45," *Arts West* vol. 8, no. 10 (November
1983), p. 20.

15.
Frances Loring
Grief   c. 1917
Bronze
Foundry Mark: "Roman Bronze Works, Inc. N.Y."
Signed: "F.N. Loring" (two times)
H. 51.0 cm
Art Gallery of Ontario, Toronto, Anonymous Gift, 1976

EXHIBITIONS: 1918 RCA AGT #196; 1925 "British Empire Exhibition, Canadian Section of Fine Arts," Wembley, England; 1928 SSC AGT #114; 1929 "Little Pictures by members of the OSA" #178; 1929 SSC NGC #56; 1932 "All Canadian Exhibition" VAG #226; 1936–7 SSC #15; 1959 CNE; 1963 "Master Canadian Painters & Sculptors," LPLAM & 1964 Sarnia Public Library & Art Gallery #28; 1966 Pollock Gallery; 1969 Pollock Gallery

LITERATURE: Ill. B. Brooker, ed., "Sculpture in Canada," in *Yearbook of the Arts in Canada 1928–9*, Plate VII.

16.
Frances Loring
A Dream Within a Dream   c. 1917 (model)
Marble
H. 62.0 cm
Collection of Georgina Public Library,
Keswick, Ontario

EXHIBITIONS: 1917 OSA #177a; 1917 WAA;
1924 "Summer Exhibition of Canadian Art,"
AGT #157; 1927 CNE #194; 1928 SSC AGT
#113; 1929 SSC NGC #50; 1932 J. Merritt
Malloney Galleries, Toronto; 1936–7 SSC #18;
1942 Print Room (marble); 1943 SSC LPLAM;
Ill. 1960 CNE

LITERATURE: Sisler, pp. 22, 63.

Carved in marble 1938–1939.

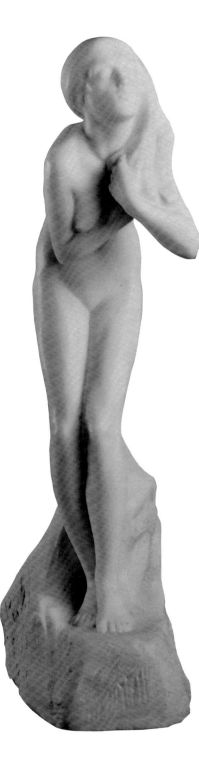

17.
Florence Wyle
Edward Kendall   c. 1918
Painted plaster relief
Signed: On verso: "Wyle Edward Kendall
1918–19"
D. 21.7 cm
Art Gallery of Ontario, Toronto, Gift of the
Estates of Frances Loring and Florence Wyle,
1983

EXHIBITIONS: 1928 SSC AGT #199; 1976 Sisler

Wyle was at the Gravenhurst Sanitarium
1917–1918; Ed Kendall was the infant son of
the doctor who treated her there.

18.
Florence Wyle
Farm Girl   1918–1919
Bronze
Foundry Mark: "Canadian Wm. A. Rogers"
H. 69.8 cm
Canadian War Museum, Canadian Museum
of Civilization, Ottawa

EXHIBITIONS: 1919 *Pictures, Sculpture,
Drawings, Etchings and Lithographs done by
Canadian Artists in Canada, under the authority
of the Canadian War Memorials Fund . . .*,
AGT #176; 1920 War Memorials #240; 1923
"Canadian War Memorials" NGC #124; 1924
"British Empire Exhibition, Canadian
Section of Fine Arts," Wembley, England
#268; 1926 War Memorials #10; 1927
"Exposition d'art canadien," Musée du Jeu de
Paume, Paris #256; 1967 "300 Years of
Canadian Art" NGC and AGT #205; 1976
"Through Canadian Eyes: Trends and
Influences in Canadian Art 1815–1965"
Glenbow-Alberta Institute #67

LITERATURE: Ill. *Canadian Art* Vol. 4, No. 1
(November–December 1946).

This figure originally held a sickle; the blade
has been separated from the figure.

19.
Florence Wyle
Noon Hour   1918–1919
Bronze
Foundry Mark: "Gorham Co. Founders"
H. 64.7 cm
Canadian War Museum, Canadian Museum
of Civilization, Ottawa

EXHIBITIONS: 1920 War Memorials #239;
1926 War Memorials #9; 1928 SSC AGT #156

LITERATURE: Ill. "War Memorial Statues,"
Mail, October 8, 1926.

20.
Frances Loring
Furnace Girl   1918–1919
Bronze
H. 61.0 cm
Canadian War Museum, Canadian Museum
of Civilization, Ottawa

EXHIBITIONS: 1920 War Memorials #205;
probably 1926 Hart House; 1926 War
Memorials #3; 1928 SSC AGT #97

21.
Frances Loring
Noon Hour at a Munitions Plant 1918–1919
Bronze relief
Foundry Mark: "Canadian Wm. A. Rogers"
88.9 × 186.7 cm
Canadian War Museum, Canadian Museum
of Civilization, Ottawa

EXHIBITIONS: 1920 War Memorials #207;
1926 Hart House; 1926 War Memorials AGT
#5; 1928 SSC AGT #92

LITERATURE: Ill. *Construction* vol. 13 (June
1920), p. 197; Ill. *Saturday Night*, vol. 34
(July 10, 1920); Ill. *Saturday Night*, vol. 53
(Oct. 15, 1938), p. 2.

22.
Florence Wyle
F.H. Varley c. 1921
Bronze
Foundry Mark: "Kristiania Kunst &
Metalstoberi, Oslo"
H. 36.7 cm
Art Gallery of Ontario, Toronto, Purchase,
Luella McCleary Endowment, 1969

EXHIBITIONS: 1922 RCA AAM #234; 1923
RCA Travelling Exhibition #115; 1923 OSA
#201; 1926 Hart House; 1927 "A Loan
Exhibition of Portraits" AGT #37; 1928 SSC
AGT #174; 1929 SSC NGC #100; 1942 Eaton's;
1962 LPLAM; 1964 "Faces of Canada: Portrait
paintings and sculptures from 1900 to the
present day," Stratford, Ontario; 1966 Pollock
Gallery; 1969 Pollock Gallery; 1983 LRAG
#51

LITERATURE: Ill. A. Jarvis, "Faces of Canada
Exhibit a Modest Social History" *Canadian
Art* Vol. 21, No. 5 (September–October
1964), p. 302; "Classic bronzes, weird
drawings, mammoth fields," *Telegram*, June
4, 1969.

An earlier bronze cast is in the collection of
the National Gallery of Canada, Ottawa.

23.
Frances Loring
Ethel Ely   c. 1921
Painted plaster
Signed: "F.N. Loring"
H. 67.0 cm
Art Gallery of Ontario, Gift of the Estates of
Frances Loring and Florence Wyle, 1983

EXHIBITIONS: 1921 OSA #178; 1922 RCA
AAM #226; 1927 "A Loan Exhibition of
Portraits" AGT #362; 1928 SSC AGT #104;
1929 SSC NGC #51; 1942 Eaton's; 1952 CNE
#25; 1966 Pollock Gallery

LITERATURE: M.O.H., "Ontario Society of
Artists constantly adding recruits," *Globe*,
March 21, 1922.

24.
Frances Loring
Marion   c. 1922
Bronze
Foundry Mark: "Canadian Wm. A. Rogers
Limited"
Signed: "F. Loring"
52.0 × 30.6 cm
Art Gallery of Ontario, Toronto, Gift of
Miss Marion Gibson, in memory of Lt. Col.
Thomson and Mrs. Gibson, Toronto, 1984

EXHIBITIONS: 1922 RCA AAM #225; 1927 "A
Loan Exhibition of Portraits" AGT #363;
1928 SSC AGT #109; 1929 SSC NGC #60

25.
Frances Loring
Madonna and Child   c. 1923
Painted plaster
Signed: "FNL"
D.25.7 cm
Mrs. R.H. Sankey, Toronto

26.
Frances Loring
Head of Woman   c. 1923
Painted plaster
H. 30.3 cm (without base)
Art Gallery of Ontario, Toronto, Gift of the
Estates of Frances Loring and Florence Wyle,
1983

for the fountain:
EXHIBITIONS: 1925 OSA #298; 1926 Hart
House; 1926 WAA; 1926 CNE #338; 1928 SSC
AGT #100; 1929 SSC NGC #65

LITERATURE: Ill. *Canadian Homes and Gardens*,
1923; Irene B. Hale "Closeup of Toronto's
Women Artists No. 1: Miss Frances Loring
and Miss Florence Wyle," *Sunday World*,
May 24, 1924; A. McFarlane, "Art Awakes
in a forgotten church," *Toronto Star Weekly*,
August 1, 1925; "Frances Norma Loring and
Notable Examples of her art in Bronze &
Stone," *Portland Sunday Telegram and Sunday
Press Herald*, November 10, 1929.

This is a cast of the head for Loring's *Mermaid
Fountain*.

27.
Florence Wyle
Ethel Ely   c. 1923
Painted plaster relief
59.0 × 37.8 cm
Art Gallery of Ontario, Toronto, Gift of the
Estates of Frances Loring and Florence Wyle,
1983

EXHIBITIONS: 1923 OSA #202; 1926 Hart
House; 1928 SSC AGT #194; 1932 J. Merritt
Malloney Galleries, Toronto; 1962 LPLAM;
1966 Pollock Gallery

28.
Florence Wyle
Mr. Ely   c. 1923
Painted plaster relief
Signed: "Wyle"
59.0 × 40.4 cm
Alan Ely, Ely Limited

EXHIBITIONS: 1928 SSC AGT #195

29.
Florence Wyle
Baby with Dolphin   c. 1923
Painted plaster
H. 106.2 cm (with base)
Art Gallery of Ontario, Toronto, Gift of the
Estates of Frances Loring and Florence Wyle,
1983

EXHIBITIONS: Ill. 1923–4 RCA NGC #199;
1926 Hart House; 1926 CNE #342 stone and
#343 bronze; 1928 SSC AGT #164; 1929
SSC NGC #103; 1938 CNE #209 stone; 1969
Pollock Gallery

LITERATURE: Ill. K. Hale, "Nymphs and Fauns
as Magic Fountains in Canadian Gardens,"
Toronto Star Weekly, August 11, 1923, p. 18.

30.
Florence Wyle
Figural Grouping (Sketch for a war
memorial)   c. 1925
Plaster
H. 14.0 cm
Art Gallery of Ontario, Toronto, Gift of the
Estates of Frances Loring and Florence Wyle,
1983

31.
Frances Loring
Figural Grouping (Sketch for a war
memorial)   c. 1925
Painted plaster
H. 24.5 cm
Art Gallery of Ontario, Toronto, Gift of the
Estates of Frances Loring and Florence Wyle,
1983

EXHIBITIONS: 1927 "Architecture and the
Allied Arts: Toronto Chapter Ontario
Association of Architects" AGT #1400

32.
Florence Wyle
Study of a Girl   c. 1926
Painted plaster
H. 55.2 cm
Art Gallery of Ontario, Toronto, Gift of the
Estates of Frances Loring and Florence Wyle,
1983

EXHIBITIONS: Ill. 1926 OSA #199; 1927 "2nd
Annual Exhibition of Canadian Art," NGC
#219; Ill. 1928 SSC AGT #166; 1929 SSC
NGC #93

NOTE: Number 32 and Number 50 bear the
same title. Number 32 is the maquette for
the larger work. As dimensions were not
indicated in the catalogue listings, their
individual exhibition histories may be confused
for later years.

Another plaster cast is in the collection of
the Montreal Museum of Fine Arts.

33.
Frances Loring
*Sketches for Osgoode Hall War
Memorial*   c. 1927
Plaster
H. 20.5 cm
Art Gallery of Ontario, Toronto, Gift of the
Estates of Frances Loring and Florence Wyle,
1983

EXHIBITIONS: 1928 SSC #124 (photograph)

LITERATURE: "War Memorial of Law Society,"
Telegram, February 7, 1928; *Mail and Empire*,
October 22, 1928.

34.
Frances Loring
Sketch for War Widow and Children   c. 1927
Painted plaster
H. 62.0 cm
Art Gallery of Ontario, Toronto, Gift of the
Estates of Frances Loring and Florence Wyle,
1983

EXHIBITIONS: 1928 SSC AGT #118; 1929 SSC
NGC #49

LITERATURE: R.E. Gesnell, "Canada's
Memorial Hall," *Saturday Night*, December 1,
1928; Josephine Hambleton, "The Memorial
Chamber Angel," Ottawa *Citizen*, November
16, 1947.

War Widow and Children was designed for the
Memorial Chamber, Parliament Buildings,
Ottawa.

35.
Florence Wyle
Totem lamp stand   c. 1927
Painted wood
H. 23.2 cm
Mr. and Mrs. Donald Ketcheson, Toronto

36.
Florence Wyle
Raven book-ends   c. 1927
H. 16.8 cm
Cast iron with paint
Marion Gibson, Toronto

EXHIBITIONS: 1930 "First Annual Exhibition of Canadian Art," Manoir Richelieu, Murray Bay, Quebec #729

37.
Florence Wyle
Owl book-ends   c. 1927
Cast iron with paint
H. 17.5 cm
Private Collection

EXHIBITIONS: 1930 "First Annual Exhibition of Canadian Art," Manoir Richelieu, Murray Bay, Quebec #728

38.
Florence Wyle
Small owl book-end   c. 1927
Cast iron with paint
H. 11.7 cm
Art Gallery of Ontario, Toronto, Gift of the Estates of Frances Loring and Florence Wyle, 1983

EXHIBITIONS: 1930 "First Annual Exhibition of Canadian Art," Manoir Richelieu, Murray Bay, Quebec #730; 1976 Sisler

LITERATURE: N. Jackson-Groves, *A.Y.'s Canada* (Toronto: Irwin, 1968), p. 164.

Numbers 38–40 were listed in the Manoir Richelieu catalogue as copies of motifs of totem poles from Kispiox, British Columbia.

39.
Florence Wyle
Indian Mother and Child   c. 1927
Painted plaster relief
Signed: "Wyle"
80.3 × 60.0 cm
Art Gallery of Ontario, Toronto, Gift of the
Estates of Frances Loring and Florence Wyle,
1983

EXHIBITIONS: 1927 "Small Pictures by members
of the OSA" AGT #254; 1928 RCA Travelling
exhibition, Imperial Art Gallery, London
#205; 1928 SSC AGT #187; 1929 SSC NGC
#105; 1930 "Little Pictures by members of the
OSA" AGT #254; 1932 J. Merritt Malloney
Galleries, Toronto; 1969 Pollock Gallery;
1977 Queen's Park

LITERATURE: William Perkins Bull, *The Perkins
Bull Collection: historical paintings by Canadian
artists illustrating pioneers and pioneering in the
County of Peel.* (Brampton: printed privately,
1934), p. 65.

40.
Florence Wyle
F.C. Loring c. 1928
Painted plaster
Signed: "W"
D. 36.0 cm
Art Gallery of Ontario, Toronto, Gift of the
Estates of Frances Loring and Florence Wyle,
1983

EXHIBITIONS: 1928 SSC AGT #188; 1929 SSC
NGC #108; 1942 Eaton's; 1969 Pollock
Gallery; 1976 Sisler Gallery; 1977 Queen's
Park

41.
Florence Wyle
Annie Savage c. 1928
Plaster relief
51.0 × 32.0 cm
Concordia Art Gallery, Montreal

EXHIBITIONS: 1928 SSC AGT #190; 1929 SSC
NGC #107

Two other casts are known to exist.

42.
Florence Wyle
Baby Fountain, Girl   c. 1928 (model)
Cast stone
97.0 × 47.5 cm
London Public Utilities Commission

EXHIBITIONS: 1928 SSC AGT #162 or #163;
1929 SSC NGC #101 or #102; 1935 SSC
AGT #256; 1935 RCA AAM #302; 1938 CNE
#210 or #211; 1942 Print Room; 1944 SSC
London; Ill. 1959 CNE "Private Collectors'
Choice in Canadian Art"

LITERATURE: Saint-Denys Garneau, *Journal
de Montréal* novembre 21–décembre 22, 1935,
p. 424; *Annual Report* of the Public Utilities
Department, 1957; Ill. "Statues for the Garden
exhibited outdoors at CNE," *Globe*, September
2, 1953; Ill. Pearl McCarthy, "Florence
Wyle's sculpture excels in the Counsell
Garden," *Globe*, August 10, 1957.

A companion piece, *Boy*, was modelled at
the same time; the stone version was cast in
1957 for the Marjorie Gibbons Counsell
Garden in Gibbons Park, London, Ontario.

43.
Florence Wyle
Portrait of Lawren Harris   c. 1928 (model)
Bronze
H. 41.7 cm
The McMichael Canadian Collection; Bequest
from the Howard K. Harris Estate

EXHIBITIONS: 1929 OSA #309; 1930 "5th
Annual Exhibition of Canadian Art," NGC
#167

LITERATURE: Ill. (plaster) *Canadian Review of
Music and Art* Vol. 3, nos. 3 & 4, 1944.

44.
Florence Wyle
Portrait of A.Y. Jackson   c. 1929
Painted plaster
Signed: "Wyle"
H. 41.0 cm
Art Gallery of Ontario, Toronto, Gift of the
Estates of Frances Loring and Florence Wyle,
1983

EXHIBITIONS: 1929 OSA #310; 1930 "5th
Annual Exhibition of Canadian Art" NGC
#168; 1966 Pollock Gallery; 1969 Pollock
Gallery; 1978 Guelph #5

45.
Florence Wyle
Young Mother   c. 1928
Bronze
Signed: "Wyle 1920" scratched into patina
H. 86.0 cm
Collection of the Sarnia Public Library and
Art Gallery, Gift of the Friends of Florence
Wyle and Frances Loring, 1964

EXHIBITIONS: 1928 50 RCA AGT #179; 1929
SSC NGC #91; 1930 "5th Annual Exhibition of
Canadian Art" NGC #169; 1930 CNE #240;
1960 "A Tribute to Women" CNE; 1976
Sisler Gallery

LITERATURE: Ill. Lenore Crawford, "Exhibition
tribute to 2 women sculptors," unsourced
clipping.

Three plaster casts are known. Wyle must
have dated this years after it was cast,
forgetting its actual date.

46.
Florence Wyle
Deer panel   c. 1929
Painted plaster
Signed: "Wyle"
87.0 × 181.2 cm
Art Gallery of Ontario, Toronto, Gift of the Estates of Frances Loring and Florence Wyle, 1983

EXHIBITIONS: 1930 "5th Exhibition of Canadian Art" NGC #170; 1930 "Little Pictures by members of the OSA" AGT #589; 1931 "An exhibition of the Toronto chapter of the Ontario Association of Architects" AGT #651; 1938 CNE #222; 1977 Queen's Park

LITERATURE: Ill. "Unique Church Studio is Home and Workshop for Loring and Wyle, Canadian Sculpture Team," *Saturday Night*, vol. 61 (November 18, 1944), p. 4; Ill. K. Clive, "The Canadian Galatea comes to life," *Canadian Homes & Gardens*, vol. 8, no. 2, (February 1931) p. 17.

47.
Florence Wyle
Small Fountainhead Frog   c. 1929
Painted plaster
H. 16.2 cm (with base)
Art Gallery of Ontario, Toronto, Gift of the Estates of Frances Loring and Florence Wyle, 1983

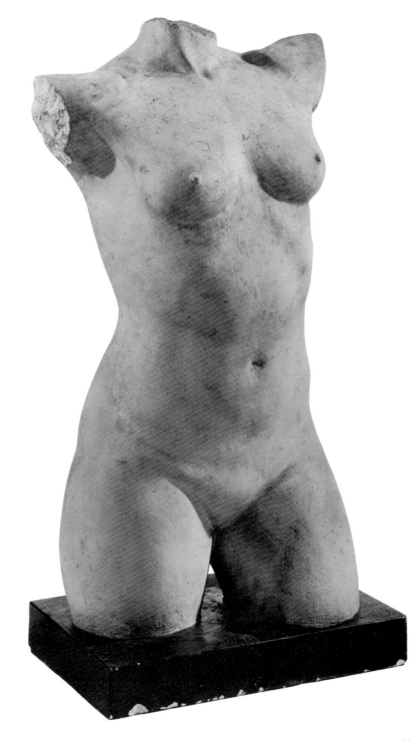

48.
Florence Wyle
Torso ("Mother of the Race")   c. 1930
Marble
H. 93.0 cm
National Gallery of Canada, Ottawa

EXHIBITIONS: 1930 CNE *#239 Torso*; 1930
RCA AGT #196; 1931 "Small Pictures by
members of the OSA" #320 (a) *Torso*; 1931
SSC NGC #34; 1932 "7th Annual Exhibition of
Canadian Art," NGC #303; 1963 "Master
Canadian Painters and Sculptors" LPLAM #48;
1966 Pollock Gallery; 1969 Pollock Gallery;
1978 Guelph #4 (plaster)

Carved by Wyle in 1932. The plaster model
is in the collection of the Art Gallery of
Ontario, Gift of the Estates of Frances Loring
and Florence Wyle, 1983.

49.
Frances Loring
Invocation c. 1930
Painted plaster
Signed: "Loring"
H. 84.0 cm
Art Gallery of Ontario, Toronto, Gift of the
Estates of Frances Loring and Florence Wyle,
1983

EXHIBITIONS: 1930 OSA AGT #257; 1931 SSC
NGC #22; 1932 J. Merritt Malloney Galleries,
Toronto; 1938 CNE #204 (in marble); 1942
Print Room; 1969 Pollock Gallery

50.
Florence Wyle
Study of a Girl c. 1931
Painted plaster
Signed: "Wyle"
H. 135.5 cm
Art Gallery of Ontario, Toronto, Gift of the
Estates of Frances Loring and Florence Wyle,
1983

EXHIBITIONS: 1931 OSA #225; 1931 CNE
#513; 1931 RCA AAM #247; 1932 "7th
Annual Exhibition of Canadian Art" NGC
#302; 1933 "8th Annual Exhibition of
Canadian Art NGC" #288; 1938 "A Century
of Canadian Art" Tate Gallery, London
#253; 1939 New York #30; 1942 Print Room;
1943 SSC London; 1950 SSC #71; 1953 CNE
#225

LITERATURE: Ill. "Canadian Sculpture makes
its first bow in U.S.," *Saturday Night*, vol.
54 (July 15, 1939), p. 17; Ill. Colgate
Canadian Art, 1943, p. 199; Ill. *Guelph
Mercury*, August 14, 1978.

See Colour Plate No. 2

51a.
Florence Wyle
Blue Heron   c. 1931 (model)
Cast stone
H. 91.5 cm (with base)
Art Gallery of Ontario, Toronto, Gift of Mr. & Mrs. D.E. Mundell, San Francisco, 1965

EXHIBITIONS: 1931 SSC NGC #39; 1938 CNE #221; 1953 CNE #221; 1961 "Exhibition and Sale of Garden Sculpture organized by the Women's Committee of the Art Gallery of Toronto" AGT #52

LITERATURE: Ill. Agnes Joynes, "The Sculptor at Work," *The Challenge*, November 8, 1936; K. Clive, "The Canadian Galatea Comes to life," *Canadian Homes & Gardens* Vol. 8, No. 2 (February, 1931), p. 17.

The stone version dates from the 1960s; one bronze was cast in 1966.

51b.
Florence Wyle
Blue Heron   c. 1931 (model)
Cast stone
H. 82.3 cm (with base)
Art Gallery of Ontario, Toronto, Gift of the Estates of Frances Loring and Florence Wyle, 1983

52.
Florence Wyle
Chicago   c. 1932
Painted plaster
Signed: "Wyle"
H. 54.0 cm
Art Gallery of Ontario, Toronto, Gift of the Estates of Frances Loring and Florence Wyle, 1983

EXHIBITIONS: 1932 SSC AGT #113; 1932 CNE #178; 1932 J. Merritt Malloney Galleries, Toronto; 1933 RCA AAM #276; 1933 "8th Annual Exhibition of Canadian Art" NGC #286; 1936 CNE #302 (bronze); 1942 Print Room NFS; 1969 Pollock Gallery

LITERATURE: Ill. "Canadian Sculptors show outstanding Work," *Globe*, April 13, 1932.

53.
Frances Loring
Girl with Fish   c. 1932
Painted plaster
H. 97.0 cm
Art Gallery of Ontario, Toronto, Gift of the Estates of Frances Loring and Florence Wyle, 1983

EXHIBITIONS: 1932 J. Merritt Malloney Galleries, Toronto *The Fish Girl*; 1933 CNE #272 *Girl with Fish Fountain*; 1933 RCA AAM #265; 1938 "A Century of Canadian Art," Tate Gallery, London #239; 1939 New York #14; 1940 WAA; 1942 Print Room; 1943 SSC London; 1948 CNE #122; 1966 Pollock Gallery; 1969 Pollock Gallery; 1978 Guelph #1; 1983 LRAG #20 (ceramic)

LITERATURE: Ill.: Paul Duval, "Smaller Works of Sculpture Belong in the Home," *Saturday Night*, vol. 61 (April 27, 1946), p. 5; Ill. "Canadian Sculpture makes its first bow in U.S.," *Saturday Night*, vol. 54 (July 15, 1939), p. 17; Ill. Colgate, *Canadian Art* (Toronto: Ryerson, 1943), p. 195.

A ceramic version is in the collection of the Woodstock Art Gallery.

54.
Florence Wyle
The Violinist   c. 1933
Painted plaster relief
D. 57.8 cm
Art Gallery of Ontario, Toronto, Gift of the
Estates of Frances Loring and Florence Wyle,
1983

EXHIBITIONS: 1933 "4th Biennial Exhibition
of Architecture and the Allied Arts by
members of the Toronto Chapter of the
Ontario Association of Architects" AGT #408;
1942 Eaton's; 1977 Queen's Park

Many copies of this exist, some with only a
single outer ring.

55.
Frances Loring
Sir Frederick Banting   c. 1934 (model)
Bronze
Foundry Mark: "Gorham Co. Founders"
H. 62.5. cm
Art Gallery of Ontario, Toronto, Gift from
the Fund of T. Eaton Co. Ltd., for Canadian
Works of Art, 1950

EXHIBITIONS: 1934 RCA AGT #205; 1935
RCA AAM #288; 1935 SSC #226; 1937
"International Society of Women Painters &
Sculptors" WAA; 1939 New York #12; 1942
Print Room; 1942 Eaton's; 1943 SSC London;
1949 CNE #23; 1953 "Silver Jubilee
Exhibition of the SSC" MMFA #48 (plaster);
1962 LPLAM; 1964 "Faces of Canada: Portrait
paintings and sculptures from 1900 to the
present day," Stratford; 1966 Pollock Gallery;
1976 "Through Canadian Eyes: Trends and
Influences in Canadian Art 1815–1965,"
Glenbow–Alberta Institute, #66; 1983 LRAG
#21

LITERATURE: Ill. *Saturday Night*, Vol. 49, no.
2, (June 16, 1934), p. 9; Ill. *Ottawa Citizen*,
March 8, 1941; Ill. *Saturday Night* (March 8,
1941); Ill. W. Abell, "Sculpture," *Studio*,
Vol. 129, no. 625 (April 1945), p. 136;
Saturday Night, Vol. 62, no. 2 (September
14, 1946); Ill. Eric Newton, *British Sculpture
1944–1946* (London: Tiranti, 1947), ill. 27;
RAIC *Journal*, Vol. 27, no. 1 (January 1950)
p. 31; *Windsor Daily Star*, October 7, 1950;
La Presse, May 24, 1951; Ill. *Saturday Night*,
June 5, 1951; *Canadian Geographical Journal*,
Vol. 43 (December 1951), p. 268; "Banting
may go to Medical Academy," *Globe*,
November 3, 1962; Ill. Alan Jarvis, "Faces of
Canada exhibit a modest social history,"
Canadian Art Vol. 21, No. 5, (September–
October 1964), p. 303; Marie Fleming,
"Sculpture: Florence Wyle, Frances Loring,"
Canadian Collector Vol. 1, No. 1, April 7,
1966; Sisler, *The Girls*, 1972, p. 55; Natalie
Luckyj, "Visions and Victories: Canadian
Women Artists 1914–45," *Arts West* vol. 8,
no No. (November 1983), p. 22.

Six bronze casts were made.

See Colour Plate No. 3

56.
Frances Loring
Goal Keeper c. 1935
Painted plaster
H. 242.0 cm
Art Gallery of Ontario, Toronto, Gift of the
Estates of Frances Loring and Florence Wyle,
1983

EXHIBITIONS: 1935 SSC #225; Ill. 1935 CNE
#251, 1938 CNE #198; 1950 CNE; 1952
Willistead Art Gallery, Windsor; 1962 LPLAM;
1964 "Faces of Canada: Portrait paintings
and sculptures from 1900 to the present day";
1969 Pollock Gallery; 1977 Queen's Park

LITERATURE: Ill. *Gossip*, Feb. 4, 1935; *Mail*,
February 22, 1935; Ill. *Canadian Life* Vol. 1,
No. 14 (Spring 1950), p. 14; Ill. *Globe
Magazine*, April 7, 1962, (cover); L. Crawford,
"Exhibit is Tribute to two Women Sculptors,"
London Free Press, 1962; Sisler, *The Girls*,
pp. 56–58; Duval, "A Monument to Don,"
Telegram, November 30, 1963.

57.
Florence Wyle
Elizabeth Wyn Wood c. 1935
Painted plaster
Signed: "Wyle"
H. 53.0 cm (with base)
Art Gallery of Ontario, Toronto, Gift of the
Estates of Frances Loring and Florence Wyle,
1983

EXHIBITIONS: 1935 SSC AGT #259; 1935 CNE
#300; 1942 SSC Eaton's; 1969 Pollock
Gallery

58.
Florence Wyle
Birdbath c. 1935
Bronze
Signed: "Wyle"
H. 139.0 cm
Private Collection

59.
Florence Wyle
Torso c. 1935
Wood
H. 36.2 cm
Collection of The Winnipeg Art Gallery.
Winnipeg Gallery and School of Art
Collection.

EXHIBITIONS: Possibly 1935 AGT #261, *Torso*,
pine

LITERATURE: Ill. Paul Duval, "Smaller Works
of Sculpture Belong in the Home," *Saturday
Night*, Vol. 61, April 27, 1946.

Many plaster versions exist in public and
private collections.

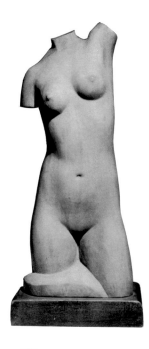

60.
Frances Loring
The Miner 1936
Painted plaster
Signed: "FN Loring 1936"
H. 81.0 cm
Art Gallery of Ontario, Toronto, Gift of the
Estates of Frances Loring and Florence Wyle,
1983

EXHIBITIONS: 1936 CNE #273 *Moose River,
1936* bronze; 1937 RCA AAM #228; 1938 SSC
AGT; 1939 New York #13; 1942 Eaton's;
1948 CNE #123; 1966 Pollock Gallery (no
No.); 1969 Pollock Gallery; 1977 Queen's
Park; 1978 Guelph #2.

LITERATURE: Sisler, p. 58; Ill. *Telegram*, March
9, 1938.

Two bronzes were cast in the 1960s when
Loring was ill.

61.
Florence Wyle
The Cellist   1937–1941
Mahogany
H. 37.5 cm
National Gallery of Canada, Ottawa

EXHIBITIONS: 1936–7 SSC Travelling Exhibition #42 plaster; 1937 "Artists of the British Empire Overseas Exhibition under Royal Charter of the Royal British Colonial Society of Artists," Royal Institute Galleries, Piccadilly, London #60 *Cellist* wood mahogany; 1938 SSC AGT; 1938 RCA AGT #254; 1939 New York #28 mahogany; 1983 LRAG #53

LITERATURE: "Canadian Sculpture makes its first bow in U.S.," *Saturday Night*, vol. 54, (July 15, 1939), p. 17; Ill. "Smaller Works of Sculpture Belong in the Home," *Saturday Night* vol. 61 (April 27, 1946) p. 5; Ill. *Canadian Art* Vol. 10, No. 4 (Summer 1953), p. 137; *Ottawa Citizen*, July 15, 1961.

This was Wyle's diploma work deposited with the RCA in 1941.

62.
Florence Wyle
Goldhamer   c. 1938
Painted plaster
H. 34.7 cm (without base)
Art Gallery of Ontario, Toronto, Gift of the Estates of Frances Loring and Florence Wyle, 1983

EXHIBITIONS: 1938 SSC AGT; 1942 SSC Eaton's

Charles Goldhamer (1903–1985) was an artist who worked primarily in watercolours. A mask also exists.

63.
Florence Wyle
American Family #1   c. 1938
Painted plaster
H. 63.7 cm
Art Gallery of Ontario, Toronto, Gift of the
Estates of Frances Loring and Florence Wyle,
1983

One of Wyle's entries for the Metropolitan
Life Insurance Company's sculpture
competition, 1938.

64.
Florence Wyle
The Harvester   c. 1938
Painted plaster
H. 114.5 cm
Art Gallery of Ontario, Toronto, Gift of the
Estates of Frances Loring and Florence Wyle,
1983

EXHIBITIONS: 1938 RCA AGT #246; 1940
CNE; 1950 CNE #27; 1956 CNE; 1966 Pollock
Gallery; 1969 Pollock Gallery; 1977 Queen's
Park; 1978 Guelph #3

This piece was posthumously cast for the
Loring-Wyle parkette, 1984, and the Donald
Forster Sculpture Park at the University of
Guelph, 1987.

65.
Frances Loring
Pigeons   c. 1938
Painted plaster
D. 64.0 cm
Mrs. R.H. Sankey, Toronto

EXHIBITIONS: 1938 SSC AGT; AGT Print Room;
1943 SSC London

LITERATURE: Sisler, pp. 62–63.

66.
Florence Wyle
Orioles   c. 1938
Plaster
64.4 cm
Art Gallery of Ontario, Toronto, Gift of the
Estates of Frances Loring and Florence Wyle,
1983

EXHIBITIONS: 1938 SSC AGT

LITERATURE: *Time Magazine*, June 21, 1950.

67.
Frances Loring
Eskimo Mother and Child c. 1938
Painted plaster
H. 190.0 cm
Art Gallery of Ontario, Toronto, Gift of the
Estates of Frances Loring and Florence Wyle,
1983

EXHIBITIONS: 1938 "A Century of Canadian
Art," Tate Gallery, London #240 (small);
1939 New York #11 (small); 1941 SSC AGT;
1942 RCA AAM & AGT #169 (in bronze);
1942 SSC Eaton's; 1943 SSC London; 1952
Willistead Art Gallery, Windsor; 1960 XXX
Biennale Internazionale d'arte, Venice #22;
1962 LPLAM; 1966 Pollock Gallery; 1969
Pollock Gallery; 1977 Queen's Park

LITERATURE: "Canadian Sculpture makes its
first bow in U.S.," *Saturday Night*, vol. 54
(July 15, 1939), p. 17; Ill. Lyn Harrington,
"Unique Church Studio is home and workshop
for Loring and Wyle, Canadian Sculpture
Team," *Saturday Night*, vol. 61 (Nov. 18,
1944), p. 5; Lyn Harrington, "Church now a
studio, gives elbow room to two industrious
sculptors," *Christian Science Monitor*, January
30,1946; Ill. *Telegram*, June 20, 1959; Ill.
L. Crawford, "Exhibit is Tribute to two women
sculptors," *London Free Press*, November
1962; *Windsor Star*, Jan. 12, 1963; "Mother
& Child Find Gallery Home," *Edmonton
Journal*, Feb. 21, 1964; Sisler, pp. 58, 108.

A stone version is in the National Gallery of
Canada; a smaller bronze is in the Edmonton
Art Gallery.

See Colour Plate No. 4

69.
Frances Loring
Study for The Brewing 1939
Plaster relief
25.5 × 27.0 cm
Art Gallery of Ontario, Toronto, Gift of the
Estates of Frances Loring and Florence Wyle,
1983

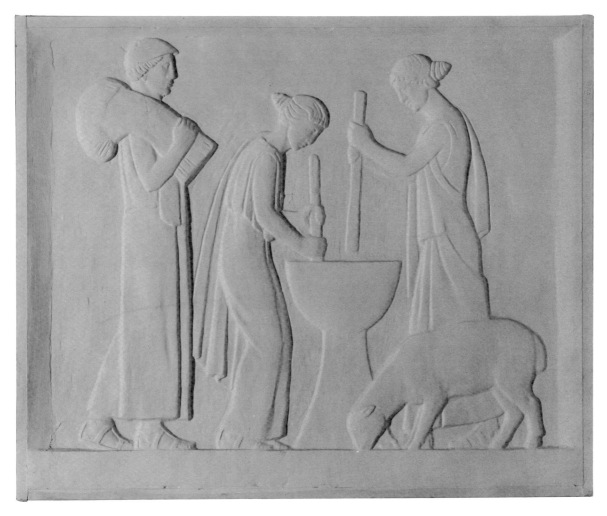

68.
Frances Loring
Beer Making in Greece: The Brewing   1939
Painted plaster
81.0 × 100.2 cm
Lawrence Hayward

EXHIBITIONS: 1941 SSC AGT

LITERATURE: B. McIntosh, "RPI gets art works in purchase of Brewery," *Daily Rye*, March 3, 1967.

One of a series of four panels made for the Board Room, O'Keefe House, now part of Ryerson Polytechnical Institute.

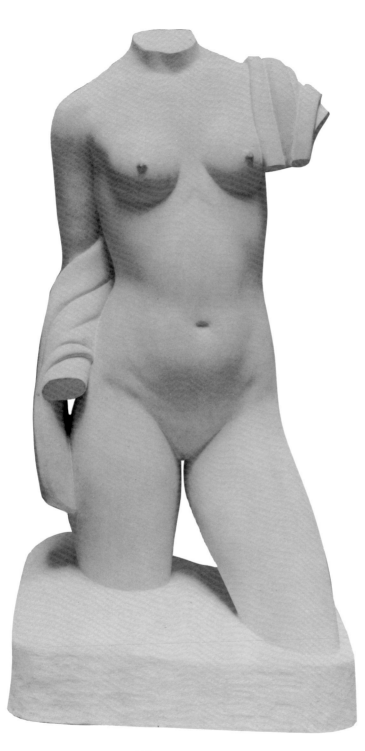

70.
Florence Wyle
Draped Torso   1939 (model)
Aur-Italian Marble
Signed: "Wyle"
H. 111.8 cm
Art Gallery of Ontario, Toronto, Gift of
Reuben Wells Leonard Estate, 1958

EXHIBITIONS: 1939 New York #29 (plaster);
1942 Print Room; 1958 SSC AGT; 1977
Queen's Park

LITERATURE: Ill. *New World Illustrated*,
February 1942, p. 28.

71.
Florence Wyle
Study for North Country   c. 1940
Plaster
Inscribed on verso: "Pine Trees/Niagara/Wyle/
Merry Christmas to Dr. & Mrs. Ormsby
Smith"
22.0 × 28.5 cm
T. Ormiston Smith, M.D.

EXHIBITIONS: 1944 SSC AGT #231; 1952 CNE
#145

LITERATURE: Pearl McCarthy, "Art & Artists,"
The Globe and Mail, August 1, 1942.

One of three reliefs for the Rainbow Bridge
Gardens. A larger more finished study was also
made and was probably the version exhibited.

72.
Florence Wyle
Bain Fountain Figure   c. 1942 (model)
Painted plaster
Signed: "Wyle"
H. 133.2 cm
Art Gallery of Ontario, Toronto, Gift of the
Estates of Frances Loring and Florence Wyle,
1983

EXHIBITIONS: Possibly 1950 SSC NGC *Fountain
Figure* Plaster; 1962 LPLAM

LITERATURE: Ill. *New World Illustrated*, February
1942; Frances Loring, "Sculpture in the
Garden," *Canadian Art* December–January
1943–4, p. 65; Ill. *Studio*, April 1945, p.
37; Elizabeth Wyn Wood, "Observations on
a Decade–1938–1948: 10 Years of Canadian
Sculpture," Journal of the *RAIC* January 1948,
p. 16; *Globe* March 24, 1951; *Ottawa Citizen*,
June 17, 1961.

73.
Florence Wyle
Nude   c. 1944
Wood
H. 44.4 cm
National Gallery of Canada, Ottawa

EXHIBITIONS: 1944 OSA #189; possibly 1944
SSC London #38

74.
Florence Wyle
Lorraine   c. 1947
White wood
H. 40.8 cm
Collection of The Winnipeg Art Gallery.
Donated by Dr. E.J. Thomas.

LITERATURE: Ill. "Sculptors would rather work
than pursue hobbies," *Telegram* August 1947,
p. 9; Ill. "Sculpture in Canada," *Canadian Life*
Vol. 1, No. 4 (Spring 1950), p. 13.

75.
Frances Loring
Dawn c.1948
Painted plaster
100.7 × 142.5 cm
Art Gallery of Ontario, Toronto; Gift of the
Estates of Frances Loring and Florence Wyle,
1983

EXHIBITIONS: 1949 SSC AGT #11 plaster NFS;
1950 Contemporary Canadian Arts #26;
1953 CNE #214

An interior relief for the Bank of Montreal
once at King and Bay streets in Toronto,
demolished in 1972.

See Colour Plate No. 6

76.
Frances Loring
Head 1948–1949
Butternut wood
H. 68.5 cm
National Gallery of Canada, Ottawa

EXHIBITIONS: 1949 SSC #9 NFS; 1949 RCA
#119; 1950 Contemporary Canadian Arts #32

LITERATURE: Ill. *Canadian Art* Vol. 6, No. 4
(Summer 1949), p. 155.

Loring's diploma work, deposited with the
RCA in 1949.

77.
Florence Wyle
The Platte   c. 1949
Sumac
Signed (underside of base): "Wyle"
H. 38.2 cm (with base)
Private Collection

EXHIBITIONS: 1949 SSC AGT #29; 1950
Contemporary Canadian Arts #68; 1962
LPLAM

LITERATURE FOR THE SERIES: Andrew Bell,
"An Exhibition of Canadian Sculpture,"
Canadian Art, Vol. 6, No. 4 (Summer 1949),
p. 156; "Contemporary Canadian Sculpture
shows more caution than experiment,"
Canadian Art Vol. VII, no. 3 (Spring 1950), p.
117; Wm S. Dale, "Sculpture," in *The Arts
in Canada: A Stock-taking at Mid-century*,
Malcolm Ross, ed., (Toronto: MacMillan,
1958), p. 38.

One of the ten original *Rivers*.

78.
Florence Wyle
The Illinois   c. 1949
Sumac
Signed: "Wyle"
Inscribed: "Illinois"
H. 36.6 cm
T. Ormiston Smith, M.D.

79.
Florence Wyle
Sleeping Cat   1949–1950
Bronze
H. 10.0 cm
Art Gallery of Ontario, Toronto, Purchase,
1963

Two bronze casts were originally made by the
artist.

80.
Florence Wyle
Sea and Shore   c. 1950 (model)
Marble
Signed: "Wyle"
H. 93.5 cm (marble)
Art Gallery of Ontario, Toronto, Gift of the
Estates of Frances Loring and Florence Wyle,
1983

EXHIBITIONS: 1950 Contemporary Canadian
Arts #287; 1950 CNE #163; 1962 LPLAM;
1966 Pollock Gallery; 1969 Pollock Gallery;
1976 Sisler; 1977 Queen's Park; 1978 Guelph
#1

Carved in marble in 1965.

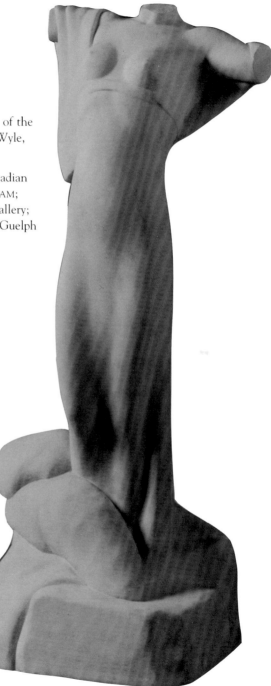

81.
Florence Wyle
Study for Little Boy Blue   1950
Painted plaster relief
Signed: "Wyle 50"
30.0 × 17.6 cm
Private Collection, Toronto

LITERATURE: Ill. Dedication Booklet, Alberta
Red Cross Crippled Children's Hospital,
Calgary, 1951.

82.
Florence Wyle
Study for Innocence   1950
Painted plaster relief
Signed: "Wyle 50"
30.0 × 17.6 cm
Private Collection, Toronto

LITERATURE: Ill. Dedication Booklet, Alberta
Red Cross Crippled Children's Hospital,
Calgary, 1951.

83.
Florence Wyle
Spring   c. 1951
Sumac
H. 35.9 cm (with base)
Mr. Jennings Young, Toronto

EXHIBITIONS: 1951 "5th Annual Sale–Paintings and sculpture by contemporary Canadian artists" AGT; 1953 Robertson Art Gallery, Ottawa #13; 1953 "7th Annual Sale of Paintings and Sculpture" AGT; 1953 McMaster University #22

"Swanee River" has been inscribed in the top; yet an estate photo of this piece bears the title "Spring," written in Wyle's hand, on the verso.

See Colour Plate No. 8

84.
Florence Wyle
Turtle   c. 1951
Painted plaster
13.0 × 23.4 cm
Art Gallery of Ontario, Toronto, Gift of the Estates of Frances Loring and Florence Wyle, 1983

EXHIBITIONS: 1951 "5th Annual Sale–Paintings and Sculpture by Contemporary Canadian artists" AGT; 1966 Pollock Gallery

85.
Florence Wyle
Summer c. 1952
Sumac
H. 38.7 cm
Catherine Thomas

EXHIBITIONS: 1952 "6th Annual Sale of paintings and sculpture" AGT

LITERATURE: Ill. Malcolm Ross, ed., *The Arts in Canada, A Stocktaking at Mid Century* (Toronto: Macmillan, 1958), p. 39.

86.
Florence Wyle
Wisdom 1953
Mahogany
H. 63.5 cm (incl. base)
Canadian Museum of Civilization, National
Museums of Canada, Gift of Theatre
Canada, Ottawa, Ontario

EXHIBITIONS: 1953 Calvert Drama Festival
Trophies AGT; 1955 CNE

LITERATURE FOR THE SERIES: *The Story of the
Calvert Trophies*; "Leading Sculptors to design
2 entries Drama Festival Trophies," *Ottawa
Journal*, January 15, 1953; Pearl McCarthy,
"Festival Trophies–a cause for rejoicing," *Globe
and Mail* March 21, 1953; *Globe* August 25,
1955; *La Presse*, January 30, 1958; "Drama
Award Wood Carving," *Sault Ste. Marie Daily
Star*, March 3, 1958; Ill. "Newest Festival
Region Faces Test this Weekend," *Globe*
February 22, 1959; Betty Lee, *Love and
Whisky*, (Toronto: Simon & Pierre Publishing
Co., 1983).

For the best presentation in the New
Brunswick Regional Festival.

87.
Florence Wyle
Drama 1953
White wood
Signed: "Wyle"
H. 81.2 cm (with base)
Canadian Museum of Civilization, National
Museums of Canada, Gift of Theatre
Canada, Ottawa, Ontario

EXHIBITIONS AND LITERATURE: see No. 86

For the best play in the finals of the Dominion
Drama Festival Competition.

88.
Frances Loring
Faun   1953
Mahogany
Signed: "Loring"
H. 63.4 cm (with base)
Canadian Museum of Civilization, National
Museums of Canada, Gift of Theatre
Canada, Ottawa, Ontario

LITERATURE: Ill. *Ottawa Journal*, October 31,
1953; *Ottawa Citizen*, Jan. 18, 1958.

For the best presentation in the Eastern
Ontario Regional Festival.

89.
Frances Loring
Invocation 1953
Mahogany
Signed: "F. Loring"
H. 64.0 cm (with base)
Canadian Museum of Civilization, National
Museums of Canada, Gift of Theatre
Canada, Ottawa, Ontario

LITERATURE: "To the Winner," Charlottetown
Patriot, March 2, 1959.

For the best presentation in the Prince Edward
Island Regional Festival.
The trophies were donated to the National
Museum of Man (now the Canadian Museum
of Civilization) in 1979 by Theatre Canada.

90.
Florence Wyle
Autumn c. 1953
Sumac
Signed: "Wyle" and inscribed underside:
"Autumn Wyle . . ."
H. 27.7 cm (with base)
Dr. and Mrs. Ben Schachter

EXHIBITIONS: 1953 "7th Annual Sale of
Paintings and Sculpture sponsored by the
Women's Committee" AGT

91.
Frances Loring
Study for Sir Robert Borden (a)   1953
Painted plaster
H. 38.0 cm
Art Gallery of Ontario, Toronto, Gift of the
Estates of Frances Loring and Florence Wyle,
1983

92.
Frances Loring
Study for Sir Robert Borden (b)   1953
Painted plaster
H. 38.0 cm
Art Gallery of Ontario, Toronto, Gift of the
Estates of Frances Loring and Florence Wyle,
1983

93.
Frances Loring
Study for Sir Robert Borden   1954
Painted plaster
H. 76.0 cm
Art Gallery of Ontario, Toronto, Gift of the
Estates of Frances Loring and Florence Wyle,
1983

EXHIBITIONS: 1957 OSA AGT; 1977 Queen's
Park

LITERATURE: "Borden–Provision for Erection
of Monument on Parliament Hill," Debates
of the House of Commons Feb. 5, 1953;
"Woman wins contest for memorial design,"
Ottawa *Citizen*, Dec. 28, 1954; *La Presse*,
Dec. 31, 1954; *Halifax Chronicle Herald* April
5, 1956; *Le Droit* Jan. 8, 1957; Ottawa
Journal, Jan. 8, 1957; "Sir Robert Comes
Back," *Weekend Magazine* vol. 7, no. 11
(1957); "Sculpture Walks: Sculpture and
Monuments in the National Capital," National
Capital Commission, 1985, p. 19.

Inscription on back reads: "Let there be no
east or west but one Canada."

94.
Frances Loring
Study for head of Sir Robert Borden   c. 1955
Painted plaster
H. 79.0 cm
Art Gallery of Ontario, Toronto, Gift of the
Estates of Frances Loring and Florence Wyle,
1983

EXHIBITIONS: 1977 Queen's Park; 1978 Guelph
#9

95.
Florence Wyle
Pauline McGibbon   1958
Signed: "Wyle 58"
Plaster
45.0 × 37.5 cm
The Honorable Pauline McGibbon

EXHIBITIONS: 1962 LPLAM; 1966 Pollock
Gallery; 1977 Queen's Park; 1976 Sisler

96.
Florence Wyle
Young Worker   c. 1958
Mahogany
34.0 × 22.5 cm
Charles McFaddin

EXHIBITIONS: 1958 "Small Pictures and
Sculpture by members of the OSA," Roberts
Gallery, Toronto

CHRONOLOGY

1881   Florence Wyle born November 24, Trenton, Illinois. Childhood spent in Waverly, Illinois.

1887   Frances Loring born October 14, Wardner, Idaho. Lived in Spokane, Washington until 1899, then in Washington, D.C., until 1900.

1900   Wyle enrolls in University of Illinois pre-med course; Loring family to Europe.

1901–03   Loring at Ecole des Beaux-arts, Geneva.

1903   Wyle transfers to School of the Art Institute of Chicago; Loring in Munich until 1904.

1904–5   Loring in Paris, Academie Colarossi.

1905   Lorings return to United States; Loring attends Art Institute of Chicago, meets Florence Wyle.

1906   Loring at School of the Museum of Fine Arts, Boston; Wyle teaches modelling at Art Institute of Chicago until 1909.

1907   Florence Wyle receives commission for marble fountain from Art Institute of Chicago.

1908   Loring in Toronto briefly.

1909–12   Loring goes to New York, settles in Macdougal Alley, soon after joined by Florence Wyle.

1912   Loring arrives in Toronto; lives at 315 Roxborough Drive; joined by Wyle early 1913; studio at 24 Adelaide Street East.

1914–20   Loring and Wyle share studio at 114½ Church Street.

1915   Sculpture exhibition at the Art Museum of Toronto.

1916   Foreign sculpture exhibition at the CNE.

1917   Loring joins WAA; does *Spirit of Canada* monumental grouping for CNE; Wyle at Gravenhurst Sanitarium suffering from respiratory problems.

1918   War Records Commission.

1919   Wyle receives comission for Memorial to Nurse Edith Cavell.

1920   Buy new home-studio, 110 Glenrose Avenue; both become members of the OSA and associates of the RCA.

1922   St. Mary Magdalene Commission.

1923   Reliefs of Evangelists' symbols for St. Anne's Church.

1924   Wyle a judge for the Wembley Exhibition; travels to London and Paris in May.

1925–26   Loring does St. Stephen War Memorial.

1926   Loring's Alpheus Todd Memorial (completed in 1928); Frances Loring becomes naturalized Canadian; Art Gallery of Toronto expansion includes Sculpture Court.

1927   Osgoode Hall War Memorial Commission given to Loring (completed in 1928); Wyle visits British Columbia to record totem poles; European sculpture exhibition at the Art Gallery of Toronto.

1928   Loring does Galt War Memorial (completed in 1930); SSC founded; *Recording Angel and War Widow* for Memorial Chamber, Parliament Buildings, Ottawa; Frances Loring to Italy (May to July); Paul Manship exhibition, Art Gallery of Toronto.

1930   Loring on Willingdon Fine Arts jury.

1932   Wyle carves *Torso* for the National Gallery; SSC charter granted.

1933   Sculptor members resign from OSA.

1936	Loring does figure of St. Michael for St. Michael's Hospital.
1937	Wyle teaches at Central Technical School during Elizabeth Wyn Wood's maternity leave.
1938	Wyle becomes RCA (first female sculptor); Oakes Pavillion Commission at Niagara Falls, Ontario; National Museum of Man record figures.
1939	SSC sends exhibit to New York World's Fair; Loring president of the WAA; Queen Elizabeth Monument.
1941	Loring and Wyle participate in the first Conference of Canadian Artists in Kingston ("the Kingston Conference"); Loring on Continuation Committee after the Conference that created the Federation of Canadian Artists.
1942	Print Room Show with Dora Wechsler and Jacobine Jones at the Art Gallery of Toronto.
1945	Wyle gives thirty-two works to the Waverly Public Library.
1947	Loring becomes RCA.
1948	Loring and Wyle reinstated to OSA; Bank of Montreal Commission.
1949	Loring visits Ivan Mestrovic in Syracuse; Wyle begins her *Rivers of America* series.
1951	Wyle works on the Alberta Children's Hospital Commission in Calgary; Loring is elected to Council of the RCA; both encourage young sculptor Frances Gage.
1952	Loring to Alberta with A.Y. Jackson on lecture tour; addition made to studio.
1953	Calvert Drama Trophies; Wyle wins Coronation medal.
1954	Loring given gold medal by University of Alberta.
1955	Loring given LLD at University of Toronto; Loring wins Borden commission.
1958	The Girls begin taking stock of their work.
1959	Wyle's *Poems* published by Ryerson Press.
1962	First retrospective of their work, held at the London Public Library and Art Museum.
1963	The Girls draw up their wills; their health begins to decline; assistance from the Friends of Loring and Wyle.
1965	Loring on City Hall Committee; Christopher Chapman films the Girls for CBC's programme *Telescope*.
1966	Loring hospitalized; retrospective at Pollock Gallery attended by Florence Wyle.
1967	The Girls transferred to Greenacres Home for the Aged, Newmarket, Ontario.
1968	Florence Wyle dies, January 13; Frances Loring dies, February 3. Memorial service and wake held.
1969	Memorial exhibition held at Pollock Gallery.
1972	Their biography, *The Girls*, by Rebecca Sisler published.
1976	Historic plaque unveiled at the studio.
1983	The Art Gallery of Ontario receives gift from the estates of Frances Loring and Florence Wyle.
1984	Loring-Wyle Parkette dedicated.

MAJOR EXHIBITIONS

1915   Sculpture exhibition, Art Museum of Toronto, November 13–December 15, 1915.

1922   Exhibition of their work at the Women's Art Association of Toronto, March 1922.

1926   Exhibition of Frances Loring and Florence Wyle, Hart House, University of Toronto, March 15–29, 1926.

1928   First exhibition of the Sculptors' Society of Canada, Art Gallery of Toronto, October 5–November 1, 1928.

1942   "In the print room: Jacobine Jones, Frances Loring, Dora Wechsler, Florence Wyle," March 6–April 5, 1942.

1952   "Sculpture by Frances Loring and Florence Wyle," Willistead Art Gallery, Windsor November 20, 1952.

1953   Exhibition at the Robertson Gallery, Ottawa, March 1953.

1953   Exhibition at McMaster University, Hamilton, November 1953.

1962   "Fifty Years of sculpture: Frances Loring and Florence Wyle. Contemporary Canadian Sculpture," London Public Library and Art Museum, London, began November 30, 1962.

1966   "Frances Loring and Florence Wyle," Pollock Gallery, Toronto, February 1966.

1969   "Frances Loring and Florence Wyle," Pollock Gallery.

1976   "Shadow of the Year," Sisler Gallery, Toronto.

1977   "Frances Loring and Florence Wyle: A Retrospective," The MacDonald Gallery, Queen's Park, Toronto, July 11, 1977–August 7, 1977.

1978   "Sculptures by Florence Wyle and Frances Loring," University of Guelph, Guelph, June 17, 1978–September 4, 1978.

SELECTED BIBLIOGRAPHY

Literature on the subject of Canadian sculpture before 1960 is minimal; therefore research for this catalogue has been based largely on the primary source materials to be found in the Public Archives of Canada in Ottawa, the Archives of Ontario, the Archives of the National Gallery of Canada and the Art Gallery of Ontario, and of various other institutions. The Loring and Wyle papers, included in the 1983 gift and presently housed in the archives of the E.P. Taylor Reference Library at the Art Gallery of Ontario, are an important resource, as is the inventory begun by Frances Gage in 1977 with a Canada Council explorations grant. This inventory, which was given to the Gallery in 1983, was intended to record as many known examples of the Girls' work as possible. The inventory provided a valuable springboard; it has been updated and supplemented as research for this exhibition progressed.

Mention should also be made of the extensive material on historical Canadian sculpture in general, and on Loring and Wyle in particular, collected by Lawrence Hayward. Copies have been deposited in both the national and provincial archives and have been consulted in both places.

In the course of research, the accuracy of dates and events had to be constantly confirmed by surveying contemporary newspapers, journals, and exhibition catalogues, since the Girls kept poor records themselves and often the dates they assigned to works in retrospect were incorrect. While one of the most rewarding aspects of this research has been contact with their friends and acquaintances whom I consulted in large numbers, unfortunately many of their most intimate friends are gone, and memories of specific details have faded. Rebecca Sisler's 1972 biography, which drew heavily on these human resources, as well as on her own personal memories fifteen years ago, will serve to round out the biographical side of the Girls' story.

CANADIAN

The Arts and Letters Club of Toronto. *The Yearbook of Canadian Art 1913*. Toronto and London: J.M. Dent, 1913.

Bakes, Alan. *Cityforms: A Biographical Supplement*. Visual Arts Ontario, 1979.

Barbeau, Marius. *Totem Poles*. Vols. 1 and 2. Ottawa: E. Cloutier, 1950–1951.

Bayer, Fern. *The Ontario Government Collection*. Markham: Fitzhenry and Whiteside, 1984.

Braide, Janet. *Anne Savage: Her expression of beauty* (exhibition catalogue). Montreal: Montreal Museum of Fine Arts, 1979.

Brooker, Bertram, et al. *Yearbook of the Arts in Canada 1928–1929*. Toronto: MacMillan, 1929.

Brown, F. Maud. *Breaking Barriers: Eric Brown and the National Gallery*. The Society for Art Publications, 1964.

Bull, William Perkins. The Perkins Bull Collection: historical paintings by Canadian artists illustrating pioneers and pioneering in the County of Peel. Brampton: printed privately, 1934.

The Canadian Who's Who. Toronto: Trans Canada Press, 1936–1937, 1948.

Castel, Jane E. "A Walking Guide to Toronto's Public Sculpture Tour A—St. Clair and Yonge." Brochure, 1985.

Catalogue of Plaster Casts, Paintings, Engravings and other Reproductions of works of art in the Museum of the Education Department, Ontario. Toronto: C. Blackett Robinson, 1884.

Chevrier, Nancy Miller. "Canadian Women

and War: A Long Tradition." *Oracle*, No. 54. National Museum of Man, 1984.

City of Toronto Planning and Development Department. *Toronto Civic Sculpture: A catalogue of the City of Toronto's Outdoor Collection*, 1985.

Colgate, William. *Canadian Art: Its Origin and Development*. Toronto: The Ryerson Press, 1943.

Dale, Wm. S.A. "Sculpture." *The Arts in Canada: A stocktaking at mid-century*. Ed. Malcolm Ross. Toronto: MacMillan, 1958.

Fairley, Barker. "At the Art Gallery," *The Rebel*. Vol. 4, No. 3 (December 1919).

Groome, L.J. "Florence Wyle—Sculptor." *The Modern Instructor: Canadian Artist Series*. June, 1958.

Hammond, M.O. *Painting and Sculpture in Canada*. Toronto: The Ryerson Press, 1930.

Hubbard, R.H. *The Development of Canadian Art*. Ottawa: National Gallery of Canada, 1963.

Hubbard, R.H. & J.R. Ostiguy. *300 Years of Canadian Art* (exhibition catalogue). Ottawa: National Gallery of Canada, 1967.

Hunt, Geoffrey. *John M. Lyle: Toward a Canadian Architecture* (exhibition catalogue). Kingston: Agnes Etherington Art Centre, 1982.

Jackson, A.Y. *A Painter's Country: The Autobiography of A.Y. Jackson*. Toronto: Clarke, Irwin, 1958.

Jones, H.G. and Edmond Dyonnet. "A History of the Royal Canadian Academy," 1934 [mimeographed copy in E.P. Taylor Reference Library, Art Galley of Ontario].

Lee, Betty. *Love and Whisky*. Toronto: Simon & Pierre, 1983.

Loring, Frances. "How to carve soap." Talk for the CBC's "Fireside Talks," in *The Red Cross Junior*. Toronto, June, 1942.

———. "How to get started: wood carving for pleasure." Toronto: Canadian YMCA War Services, in cooperation with the Canadian Legion Educational Services (1942–1943).

Luckyj, Natalie. *Visions and Victories: 10 Canadian Women Artists 1914–1945* (exhibition catalogue). London: London Regional Art Gallery, 1983.

MacCarthy, Hamilton. "The Development of Sculpture in Canada" in J. Castell Hopkins, ed., *Canada: An Encyclopaedia of the Country*, Vol. 4. Toronto: The Linscott Publishing Company, 1898.

MacDonald, Colin S. *A Dictionary of Canadian Artists*, Vol. 4. Ottawa: Canadian Paperbacks Publishing Ltd., 1974.

McDougall, Anne. *Anne Savage: The Story of a Canadian Painter*. Montreal: Harvest House, 1977.

McInnes, G. *A Short History of Canadian Art*. Toronto: MacMillan, 1939.

———. *Canadian Art*. Toronto: MacMillan, 1950.

McMann, E. de R. *The Royal Canadian Academy of Arts—L'academie royale des arts du Canada: Exhibitions and Members 1880–1979*. Toronto: University of Toronto Press, 1981.

McTavish, Newton. *The Fine Arts in Canada*. Toronto: MacMillan, 1925.

———. *Ars Longa*. Toronto: The Ontario Publishing Company Limited, 1938.

The Municipal Review of Canada. *War Memorials Souvenir Number*. Montreal: Municipal Publishing Company Ltd. of Canada, 1925.

National Capitol Commission Visual Arts Programme. "Sculpture Walks: Sculptures and Monuments in the National Capitol." Ottawa: NCC, 1985.

Pantazzi, S. "Foreign art at the CNE 1905–1938." NGC *Bulletin*, 22/1973.

Porter, John R. and Jean Bélisle. *La Sculpture ancienne au Québec: Trois siècles d'art religieux et profane*. Montréal: Les éditions de l'homme, 1986.

Report of the Royal Commission on National Development in the Arts, Letters and Sciences. Ottawa: E. Cloutier, 1951.

Robertson, Heather. *A Terrible Beauty: The Art of Canada at War*. Toronto: James Lorimer, 1977.

Shipley, Robert. "To mark our place." Unpublished manuscript, 1984.

Sisler, Rebecca. *The Girls: A Biography of Frances Loring & Florence Wyle*. Toronto: Clarke, Irwin, 1972.

Stacey, R.H., ed. "Lives and Works of the Canadian Artists." No. 18: Frances Loring; No. 20: Florence Wyle. Toronto: Dundurn Press, 1978.

Walker, Hugh. *The Spencer Clark Collection of Historic Architecture*. Scarborough: Guildwood Hall, 1982.

Who's Who in Ontario Art. The Ontario Library Review, 1948.

Wodehouse, R.F. *Checklist of the War Collections*. Ottawa: The National Gallery of Canada, 1968.

Wyle, Florence. *Poems*. Toronto: The Ryerson Press, 1959.

General Sculpture

Armstrong, Tom, et al. *200 Years of American Sculpture* (exhibition catalogue). New York: Whitney Museum of American Art, 1976.

Bartlett, Paul W. "What American sculptors owe to French art," *New York Times*, February 9, 1913.

Bogart, Michele H. and Deborah Nevins. *Fauns and Fountains: American Garden Statuary 1890–1930* (exhibition catalogue). Southampton, New York: The Parrish Art Museum, 1985.

Casson, Stanley. *20th Century Sculptors*. London: Oxford University Press, 1930.

Churchill, Allen. *The Improper Bohemians: A Recreation of Greenwich Village in its Heyday*. New York: E.P. Dutton, 1959.

Craven, Wayne. *Sculpture in America* (rev. ed.). Newark: University of Delaware Press, 1984.

Dallin, Cyrus E. "American Sculpture: its present aspects and tendencies," *Brush and Pencil*, Vol. 2, No. 6 (March 1903).

Elsen, Albert E. et al. *Rodin Rediscovered*. Washington: National Gallery of Art, 1981.

Elsen, Albert E. *The Partial Figure in Modern Sculpture: From Rodin to 1969*. Baltimore: The Baltimore Museum of Art, 1969.

Encyclopaedia Britannica, 11th ed., Vol. 24, "Sculpture," 1910–1911.

Farnsworth, P.T. "The Artists' Colony in Macdougal Alley, where some of our best known painters and sculptors live and work," *The Craftsman*, Vol. 11, No. 1 (October 1906).

Fusco, Peter and H.W. Janson, eds. *The Romantics to Rodin: French Nineteenth Century Sculpture from North American Collections*. Los Angeles: Los Angeles County Museum of Art, 1980.

Gilmore, Roger, ed. *Over a Century: A History of the School of the Art Institute of Chicago 1866–1981*. Chicago: The School of the Art Institute of Chicago, 1982.

Goldman, Emma. *Living My Life*. Vols. 1 and 2. New York: Dover Publishing, 1970. (Reprint of 1931 edition.)

Greenthal, Kathryn. *Augustus Saint-Gaudens: Master Sculptor*. New York: The Metropolitan Museum of Art, 1985.

Hill, May Brawley. *The Woman Sculptor: Malvina Hoffman and her Contemporaries* (exhibition catalogue). New York: Berry-Hill Galleries, 1984.

International Business Machines Corporation. *Sculpture of the Western Hemisphere: Permanent Collection of the International Business Machines Corporation*, 1942.

Mirolli, Ruth. *Nineteenth Century French Sculpture: Monuments for the Middle Class* (exhibition catalogue). Louisville: J.B. Speed Museum, 1977.

Newton, Eric. *British Sculpture 1944–46*. London: John Tiranti, 1947.

Nochlin, Linda. "Malvina Hoffman: A Life in Sculpture," *Arts Magazine*, Vol. 59, No. 3 (November 1984), pp. 106–110.

Parkes, K. *Sculpture of Today*. Vol. 1: *America, Great Britain, Japan*; Vol. 2: *Continent of Europe*. Universal Art Series. London: Chapman and Hall, 1921.

Pingeot, Anne et al. *La Sculpture française au XIXe siècle* (exhibition catalogue). Paris: Galeries nationales du Grand Palais, 1986.

Rather, Susan. "The Past made modern: Archaism in American Sculpture," *Arts Magazine*, Vol. 59, No. 3 (November 1984).

Rubinstein, Charlotte Streifer. *American Women Artists from Early Indian Times to the Present*. Boston, G.K. Hall, 1982.

Scudder, Janet. *Modelling my Life*. New York: Harcourt, Brace, 1925.

Sparkes, Esther. "A Biographical Dictionary of Painters and Sculptors in Illinois 1808–1945," PhD Dissertation for Northwestern University, 1971.

Taft, Loredo. *The History of American Sculpture*. Arno Press, 1969 (reprint of 1924 MacMillan edition).

Vollmer, H. *Kunstler Lexikon des Zwanzigsten Jahrhunderts*. Leipzig: Veb E.A. Seemann, 1956.

Wasserman, Jeanne L., ed. *Metamorphosis in Nineteenth Century Sculpture* (exhibition catalogue). Cambridge: Fogg Art Museum, 1975.

Weimann, Jeanne M. *The Fair Women: The Story of the Woman's Building, World's Columbian Exposition, Chicago, 1893*. Chicago: Academy Chicago, 1981.

Weller, Allen S. "Lorado Taft," Bulletin of the Krannert Art Museum, Vol. 8, No. 2, 1983.

———. *Lorado in Paris: The Letters of Lorado Taft 1880–1885*. Urbana and Chicago: University of Illinois Press, 1985.

Wilson, Richard Guy, et al. *The American Renaissance 1876–1917* (exhibition catalogue). New York: The Brooklyn Museum, 1979.

PERIODICAL LITERATURE

1906 Taft, Lorado. "Exhibition of Statuary, Art Institute, Chicago," *The Sketchbook*, Vol. 5, No. 10 (August 1906).

1911 "Girl Depicts Dreams in Marble and Bronze: Gotham Sculptor enters Spokane Contest," *Denver Colorado News*, August 22, 1911.

Bennett, Helen Christine. "Child Figures in Fountains: Good modeling and faithful portrayal of child spirit characteristic of Florence Wyle's work," *Arts and Decoration*, Vol. 1, February, 1911.

"Sculpture important in the National Academy Exhibition for the Winter of 1910," *The Craftsman*, Vol. 19, No. 5 (February, 1911).

1912 Haswell, E.B. "The 16th Annual exhibition of the Society of Western Artists," *The International Studio*, Vol. 47, No. 186 (August 1912).

1914 Kerr, Estelle M. "Women Sculptors in Toronto," *Women's Saturday Night* (June 21, 1914).

1915 "Local artists show sculptory: Splendid exhibition is now on view at the Grange," *Mail*, November 27, 1915.

"Toronto sculptors spring a surprise," *Globe*, November 15, 1915.

1917 "Miss Canada in Yonge Street: Heroic Figure of Lady of Confederation in front of T. Eaton Co. Store," the *Globe*, June 30, 1917.

1920 Merrill, Anne. "The Average Woman," *Mail and Empire*, September 4, 1920.

"Novel Studio for Sculptors," *Mail and Empire*, November 20, 1920.

"Turn unused Church into sculptors' studio," *Star*, November 27, 1920.

1921 "A Beautiful Memorial Recently Revealed," *Saturday Night*, April 23, 1921.

"Can't get very far without hard work: Success secret of young sculptress who modelled Cavell Memorial Tablet," *Star Weekly*, August 27, 1921.

1922 "The Rood at St. Mary Magdalen's (Anglican) Church, Toronto," *Saturday Night*, March 11, 1922.

1923 "Native sculpture in Canadian Galleries," *Saturday Night*, January 13, 1923.

Katherine Hale, "Nymphs and Fauns as Magic Fountains in Canadian Gardens," *Toronto Star Weekly*, August 11, 1923.

1924 Hare, Irene B. "Closeups of Toronto's Women Artists: No. 1 Miss Frances Loring and Miss Florence Wyle," *Sunday World*, May 25, 1924.

"Canadian Sculpture to the Fore," *Saturday Night*, September 6, 1924.

1925 Wyle, Florence. "An inspiring memorial that is needed at home," the *Globe*, April 2, 1925. Letter to the editor.

"National Monument designed in Toronto," the *Star*, July 17, 1925.

Mcfarlane, Arthur. "Art Awakes in a Forgotten Church," *Toronto Star Weekly*, August 1, 1925.

1926 "Vigor and Fine Taste Seen in work of Local Sculptors: Exhibition by Florence Wyle and Frances Loring in Hart House Sketch Club Reveals Marked Progress of Delicate Art in Canada," *Globe and Mail*, March 23, 1926.

"The Toronto Art Gallery: New Extensions to be opened shortly bring it to Metropolitan Dimensions," *Saturday Night*, January 9, 1926.

1927 Dunington-Grubb, L.A. "Sculpture as Garden Decoration," *Canadian Homes and Gardens*, March, 1927.

Lyle, John M. "The Allied Arts at the Recent Toronto Chapter Exhibition," RAIC *Journal*, May, 1927.

"Daring Canadian Girl in an Indian Village: Miss Florence Wyle of Toronto Models Totem Poles for Government," *Daily Star*, September 10, 1927.

1928 Charlesworth, Hector. "Contemporary Canadian Sculpture," *Saturday Night*, October 27, 1928.

"Law Society Memorial," the *Star*, November 7, 1928.

"War Memorial of Law Society," the *Telegram*, February 7, 1928.

"Beautiful war memorial which is favored for Galt," *Galt Evening Reporter*, November 10, 1928.

"In memory of law society members who lost their lives," *Globe*, October 22, 1928.

"Big Crowds, Seven Shows as Art Gallery Reopens," the *Star*, October 1928.

Gosnell, R.E. "Canada's Memorial Hall," *Saturday Night*, December 1, 1928.

"Frances Loring back from trip to Italy: spent three months there executing war memorial for Law Society," *Star*, August 28, 1928.

1929 "Frances Norma Loring and Notable Examples of her art in Bronze and Stone," *Portland Sunday Telegram and Sunday Press Herald*, November 10, 1929.

1930 Salinger, Jehanne Bietry. "Women Sculptors Prominent at OSA: Superior sculpture present but rare at 58th exhibition," *Mail*, March 22, 1930.

1931 Clive, Katharine. "The Canadian Galatea comes to life: The development of a national movement in art and decoration," *Canadian Homes and Gardens*, February 1931.

"Three Artists join in Exhibit of Recent Work," *Montreal Gazette*, November 18, 1931.

McCarthy, Pearl. "Works of Ontario Artists Display Catholicity," *Mail*, March 7, 1931.

1932 "Sculpture—Canvas exhibit by five Canadian Women: Malloney Gallery shows notable assembly of exquisite pieces," *Mail*, December, 1932.

McCarthy, P. "Canadian Sculptors achieve distinction: Exhibition at Art Gallery provides creditable standard 54 pieces shown," *Mail*, April 8, 1932.

Joynes, A. "Among Canadian Sculptors: Florence Wyle ARCA," clipping, November 27, 1932 (no source).

"Canadian Sculptors show outstanding work," the *Globe*, April 13, 1932.

1934 "Harmony in art is emphasized by Miss Loring," *Globe*, February 15, 1934.

1936 Joynes, Agnes. "The Sculptor at Work," *The Challenge*, November 8, 1936.

1938 Joynes, Agnes. "Loring the Sculptor," *Saturday Night*, October 15, 1938.

McInnes, Graham. "A century of Canadian Art Exhibition at the Tate Gallery, London," *The Studio*, Vol. CXVI, No. 549, December, 1938.

"Florence Wyle, New RCA, Finds Abandoned Church is Ideal Studio," *Montreal Gazette*, November 28, 1938.

Hunter, Louis V. "New Woman Academician has her Studio in an Abandoned Church," *Ottawa Evening Citizen*, November 24, 1938.

"Dreams in Stone," *Toronto Star Weekly*, May 14, 1938.

Hunter, Louis V. "Her Studio in small unused Toronto Church," *Timmins Press*, November 26, 1938.

Arthur, Eric. "Sculpture in Building," RAIC *Journal*, Vol. 15, No. 6 (June 1938).

1939 "Canadian Sculpture makes its first bow in U.S.," *Saturday Night*, July 15, 1939.

1942 "Canadian Sculptors plan demonstration of modelling of head," *London Evening Free Press*, May 8, 1942.

Bridle, A. "Work of 4 Women in Sculpture show," *Star*. March 13, 1942.

"Women with Mallets: Loring and Wyle complete three decades of partnership in sculpture," *New World Illustrated*, February, 1942.

Conde, Valerie. "Canadian Sculptors," Windsor *Star*, April 4, 1942.

McCarthy, P. "Art and Artists," *Globe and Mail*, August 13, 1942.

"Lecture given by sculptress," *London Free Press*, May 11, 1942.

1943 Loring, Frances. "Sculpture in the Garden," *Canadian Art*, Vol. 1, No. 2 (December–January 1943–1944), pp. 64–67.

"Says good education is important for artist," *London Evening Free Press*, April 14, 1943.

1944 Harrington, Lyn. "Unique Church Studio is Home and Workshop for Loring and Wyle, Canadian Sculpture Team," *Saturday Night*, November 18, 1944.

1945 "The Story of a Waverly Artist," *Waverly Journal*, December 21, 1945.

Abell, Walter. "Sculpture," *The Studio* (Special Canadian Issue), Vol. 119, No. 625 (April 1945).

1946 Duval, Paul. "Smaller Works of Sculpture belong in the Home," *Saturday Night*, April 27, 1946.

Harrington, Lyn. "Church, now a studio, gives elbow room to two industrious sculptors: Loring-Wyles use big space for vast work," *Christian Science Monitor*, January 30, 1946.

Wuorio, Eva-Lis. "Sculpture a lifetime job, View of Frances Loring," *Globe*, June 1, 1946.

"Noted Artist puts life into stone and bronze," *Canadian Tribune*, June 15, 1946.

1947 Hambledon, Josephine. "The Memorial Chamber Angel," *Ottawa Citizen*, November 11, 1947.

"Canadian Panorama in Carvings for New Bank Building Here," *Globe and Mail*, April 16, 1947.

"Sculptors would rather work than pursue hobbies," the *Telegram*, August 1, 1947.

1948 McCarthy, P. "Sculpture to enhance busy street," *Globe and Mail*, May 22, 1948.

Wood, Elizabeth Wyn. "Observations

on a Decade: 1938–48: Ten Years of Canadian Sculpture," RAIC *Journal*, January, 1948.

Brown, Bill. "Stone Story: Sculpture project enhances Toronto's business district," *Montreal Standard*, 1948.

"Stone figures by Toronto Sculptors blend Canadian themes in Bank Building," *Globe*, September 3, 1948.

"Right Statuary in the Garden is Important," *London Free Press*, September 18, 1948.

"Sculptors tell Canada's Story in Bank's Stone Carvings," the *Evening Telegram*, September 18, 1948.

1949 McCarthy, Pearl. "Bank of Montreal Panels soon adopted by citizens," *Globe and Mail*, September 3, 1949.

Horne, Cleeve. "Bank of Montreal Building, Toronto . . . and Sculpture," RAIC *Journal*, Vol. 26, No. 11 (November 1949).

Hambledon, Josephine. "Canadian Women Sculptors," *Dalhousie Review*, Vol. 29, No. 3 (October 1949).

Bell, Andrew. "An Exhibition of Canadian Sculpture," *Canadian Art*, Vol. 6, No. 4 (Summer 1949).

Vickers, G. Stephen. "The Architecture in Sculpture," RAIC *Journal*, Vol. 26, No. 1 (January 1949), pp. 28–31.

1950 Bell, Andrew. "Sculpture in Trees: A successful innovation," *Canadian Art*, Vol. 8, No. 2 (Christmas 1950).

"Frances Loring, sculptor, gives interesting talk on art," *Ottawa Evening Journal*, February 8, 1950.

"Sculptor gives interesting talk on art," *Ottawa Citizen*, February 8, 1950.

"Sculpture in Canada," *Canadian Life*, Vol. 1, No. 4 (Spring 1950).

"Contemporary Canadian Sculpture shows more caution than experiment," *Canadian Art*, Vol. 7, No. 3 (Spring 1950).

1951 "Sculpture in Canada," *Canadian Geographic Journal*, Vol. 43 (December 1951).

1952 "Sculptor plans exhibit talk: Miss Frances Loring will give lecture," Windsor *Daily Star*, November 20, 1952.

"Jackson, Loring to speak in North," Lethbridge *Herald*, October 2, 1952.

"Distinguished Woman Sculptor Here," Edmonton *Journal*, October 16, 1952.

"Loring, Wyle Sculpture," Windsor *Daily Star*, December 6, 1952.

"Three Elements in Sculpture: Line and Form, Mood and Silence Needed," Windsor *Daily Star*, November 21, 1952.

1953 Carrington, Lyn. "Sculptures form Fine Exhibition," *London Free Press*, January 13, 1953.

Harrington, Lyn and Richard Harrington. "Living with Sculpture," *Family Herald and Weekly Star*, June 18, 1953.

"Leading Sculptors to design Drama Festival Trophies," Ottawa *Journal*, January 15, 1953.

McCarthy, P. "Festival Trophies—A Cause for Rejoicing," *Globe and Mail*, March 21, 1953.

————. "New Sculpture at OVC sets an example of service," *Globe and Mail*, December 5, 1953.

1954 McCarthy, P. "Contest-winning Sculptor to model fighting Borden," *Globe and Mail*, December 29, 1954.

"Gave Demonstration: Famed Canadian sculptress at Brantford Art League," Brantford *Expositor*, March 9, 1954.

McCarthy, P. "Sculptor offered award for service to Arts," *Globe and Mail*, June 21, 1954.

"Toronto Three win awards of Alberta University," *Globe and Mail*, June 29, 1954.

1955 Aitken, M. "Between you and me," the *Telegram*, October 28, 1955.

"Sculptress awarded LLD at Varsity Graduation," the *Star*, May 30, 1955.

McCarthy, Pearl. "Art Association honors noted sculptor," *Globe and Mail*, October 13, 1955.

"Frances Loring a gagné le concours," *Le Droit*, January 20, 1955.

"Frances Loring and her dreams," *CBC Times*, July 22–28, 1956.

1957 "Sir Robert comes back to Parliament Hill," *Weekend Magazine*, Vol. 7, No. 11, 1957.

McCarthy, P. "New Plastic Material in a Loring Sculpture," *Globe and Mail*, June 29, 1957.

————. "Art is Everywhere," *Globe and Mail*, May 4, 1957.

————. "Florence Wyle's Sculpture Excels in the Counsell Garden," *Globe and Mail*, August 10, 1957.

Moodie, Sheila. "Noted Toronto Sculptress finds Canada a Challenge," *Ottawa Citizen*, January 10, 1957.

1959 "Support for sculptors urged in gallery panel," Ottawa *Citizen*, May 20, 1959.

"Frances Loring: Canada's Grand Dame of Sculpture," *Kitchener-Waterloo Record*, May 16, 1959.

Usher, Edna. "We're all in debt to these women," *Telegram*, April 25, 1959.

"Dr. Frances Loring urges public support of art," Ottawa *Journal*, November 10, 1959.

1960 Lewis, John R. "Why would a woman want to be sculptor?" *Star Weekly Magazine*, January 2, 1960.

"Sculptor issues call for support," Kitchener-Waterloo *Record*, January 16, 1960.

1961 McCarthy, P. "Her hope: To die standing," *Globe and Mail*, December 16, 1961.

1962 Jarvis, A.H., ed. "Sculpture in Canada," *Canadian Art*, Vol. 19, No. 80 (July–August 1962).

Kritzwiser, K. "Hands that mold beauty," *Globe Magazine*, April 7, 1962.

Crawford, L. "Exhibit is Tribute to Two Women Sculptors," *Globe and Mail*, November 3, 1962.

———. "Dr. Comfort opens 2-sculptor show," London *Free Press*, November 10, 1962.

1963 Crawford, L. "Fifty years of sculpture: Loring and Wyle at the London Public Library and Art Museum," *Canadian Art*, Vol. XX, No. 2 (March–April 1963).

"Fund for Sculptors who helped others," *Globe and Mail*, September 28, 1963.

Parr, Roger P. "The Uses of Simplicity," *Country Beautiful*, Vol. 2, No. 8, May 1963.

Duval, Paul. "A Monument to Don," *Telegram*, November 30, 1963.

Saltmarche, Kenneth. "Sculpture Exhibit," Windsor *Star*, January 12, 1963.

1964 Jarvis, Alan. "Faces of Canada Exhibit a Modest Social History," *Canadian Art*, Vol. 21, No. 5 (September–October 1964).

"Mother and Child find Gallery Home," Edmonton *Journal*, February 21, 1964.

"Love Affair pays off!" Sarnia *Gazette*, January 30, 1964.

1965 Munk, Linda. "A talk with Miss Loring and Miss Wyle," *Globe and Mail*, May 6, 1965.

"Telescope will visit sculptors," Halifax *Chronicle-Herald*, May 1, 1965.

1966 Fleming, Marie. "Sculpture: Florence Wyle, Frances Loring," *Canadian Collector*, Vol. 1, No. 1 (April 1966).

1967 Thomson, Hugh. "Loring-Wyle influence lives on in sculpture," *Globe and Mail*, April 8, 1967.

"Whatever happened to Frances Loring and Florence Wyle," *Telegram*, March 17, 1967.

1968 "The Girls," editorial in the *Globe and Mail*, February 7, 1968.

Kritzwiser, K. "Valedictory in Studio Church," *Globe and Mail*, February 2, 1968.

"Frances Loring: A constant contributor to sculpture," *Globe and Mail*, February 6, 1968.

"Famed sculptress dies at eighty," *Telegram*, February 6, 1968.

"Canadian Sculptor Frances Loring dies," Ottawa *Journal*, February 6, 1968.

"Miss Loring a laissé un oeuvre considérable," *La Presse*, February 8, 1968.

"The Girls," editorial, *Globe and Mail*, February 7, 1968.

1969 Adilman, Sid. "It was the salon of Canada's art world, but time seems to have passed it by," *Telegram*, February 1, 1969.

Andrews, B. "Classic Bronzes, weird drawings, mammoth fields," *Telegram*, June 4, 1969.

Kritzwiser, K. "The Girls show to foster young talent," *Globe and Mail*, June 2, 1969.

1971 "QEW widening costs lion his post," the *Star*, June 18, 1971.

1973 Cherry, Zena. "After a Fashion," *Globe and Mail*, April 24, 1973.

"The Girls," *Globe and Mail*, April 24, 1973.

Mackenzie, Susan. "Forgotten treasures grace public squares," Kitchener-Waterloo *Record*, April 21, 1973.

1974 "Old Monument in New Spot," the *Star*, August 27, 1974.

1975 Cherry, Zena. "Parked Lion," *Globe and Mail*, August 5, 1975.

McLennan, Gordon. "Loring and Wyle to be re-released after ten years," *Art Magazine*, Vol. 7, No. 24 (December–January 1975).

1976 Kritzwiser, Kay. "Homage to Hands in slender handset book," *Globe and Mail*, April 7, 1976.

1977 McKinley, B. "The Art Scene," *Sun*, July 10, 1977.

1978 "Sculptures by Florence Wyle and Frances Loring at U. of G.," Guelph *Mercury*, August 14, 1978.

1980 "Pauline McGibbon unveils sculpture," *Globe and Mail*, May 7, 1980.

1983 Luckyj, N. "Visions and Victories: Canadian Women Artists 1914–1945," *ArtsWest*, Vol. 8, No. 10 (November 1983).

Rooney, Frances. "Loring and Wyle, Sculptors," *Pink Ink*, Vol. 1, Issue I (July 1983).

Jones, Donald. "Loring-Wyle Memorial Park honors odd-couple sculptors," *Toronto Star*, June 18, 1983.

1985 Dault, Gary Michael. "This City: Artists in Residence," *Toronto Life*, August 1985.

Rooney, Frances. "Frances Loring and Florence Wyle, Sculptors," *Resources for Feminist Research*, Vol. 13, No. 4 (December–January 1984–1985).

"Curator seeks works for exhibit," *Globe and Mail*, October 26, 1985.

PHOTO CREDITS

Note: Original photographs that were part of the gift of the estates of Frances Loring and Florence Wyle, 1983 are located in the Edward P. Taylor Reference Library, Art Gallery of Ontario.

Art Gallery of Ontario Cat. Nos. 1, 4, 5, 6, 7, 8, 9, 10, 11, 15, 16, 17, 22, 23, 24, 25, 26, 27, 28, 29, 30, 31, 32, 33, 34, 35, 36, 37, 38, 39, 40, 42, 44, 45, 46, 47, 49, 50, 51a, 51b, 52, 53, 54, 55, 56, 57, 58, 59, 60, 62, 63, 64, 65, 66, 67, 68, 69, 70, 71, 72, 75, 77, 78, 79, 80, 81, 82, 83, 84, 86, 87, 88, 89, 90, 91, 92, 93, 94, 95, 96; Figures 1, 4, 6, 8, 9, 10, 11, 12, 13, 17, 19, 23, 26, 31, 32, 35, 36, 42, 44, 45, 46, 51, 54, 57; Colour Plate Nos. 2, 3, 4, 6, 8

National Gallery of Canada, Ottawa: W. Hartmann: Cat. Nos. 2, 14, 48, 61, 73

National Gallery of Canada: Cat. No. 76, Figure 18

London Regional Art Gallery: Cat. No. 3

Public Archives of Canada, Ottawa: Cat. Nos. 12, 13

Canadian War Museum, Canadian Museum of Civilization, Ottawa: Cat. Nos. 18, 19, 20, 21

Concordia Art Gallery, Concordia University, Montreal: Cat. No. 41

The McMichael Canadian Collection, Kleinburg: Cat. No. 43

Sarnia Public Library and Art Gallery: Cat. No. 45

The Winnipeg Art Gallery: Ernest Mayer: Cat. Nos. 59, 85

The Winnipeg Art Gallery: Sheila Spence: Cat. No. 74

Jean Gainfort Merrill: Figures 28, 55

Herb Nott: Figures 25, 43, 47

Nott and Merrill: Figure 39

Everett Roseborough: Figure 53

Gilbert Milne: Figures 49, 50

Dennis Colwell: Figure 40

Pringle and Booth Limited: Figures 3, 24, 30, 33, 34, 56

Archives, Eaton's of Canada: Figures 20, 21

Standard Photo Illustrating Company, New York: Figures 14, 15

M.O. Hammond: Figures 7, 27

Christies, New York: Figure 16

The Metropolitan Museum of Art, New York: Figure 2

Museum of Fine Arts, Boston: Figure 5

James Chambers: Figures 22, 29, 37, 38, 48, 59; Colour Plate Nos. 1, 5

Larry Ostrom: Figures 40, 41, 58

Royal Ontario Museum, Toronto: Figure 52

Editor: Charis Wahl

Graphic Design: Steve Boyle

Composition: Q Composition Inc.

Colour Separations: Litho Plus Inc.

Printing: MacKinnon-Moncur Ltd.

Set in Goudy Old Style and printed on
Warrens Lustro Dull.